ALICELAND

A Guide to Ease

Living with Dis-Ease

by Alice Pesta

www.4thfloorpress.com

©2019 Alice Pesta

All rights reserved. No part of this publication may be reproduced in any form or by any means without the express prior written consent of the publisher and/or author, other than short excerpts (200 words or less) for reviews.

THIS BOOK IS COMPRISED OF THE AUTHOR'S PERSONAL MEMORIES, EXPERIENCES, AND INSIGHTS. THIS BOOK IS NOT INTENDED AS A SUBSTITUTE FOR THE MEDICAL ADVICE OF PHYSICIANS. THE READER SHOULD REGULARLY CONSULT A PHYSICIAN IN MATTERS RELATING TO HIS/HER PHYSICAL AND MENTAL HEALTH.

ISBN 978-1-988993-20-1

4th Floor Press, Inc.
www.4thfloorpress.com
1st Printing 2019

As a recipient of two kidney transplants and countless blood transfusions during various medical procedures, I would like to express my heartfelt gratitude to:

- all organ donors and prospective organ donors who have signed their organ transplant consents;
- all blood donors;
- doctors, nurses and other medical practitioners everywhere;
- everyone who supported me in my transformation and,
- most notably, my family and friends.

Thank you.

CONTENTS

Foreword	1
MY STORY	3
THOUGHT	12
The Three Cs of Aliceland	19
The First C of Aliceland	21
CHANCE	22
RECOGNIZE	22
BE WISE	41
LEARN	43
THE MIND	52
The Second C of Aliceland	54
CHOICE	55
HONOR YOUR CHOICE	60
HABITS	65
GRACE-BLESSING-RELEASE	70
WHO YOU THINK YOU ARE	77
EMPTINESS	92
The Third C of Aliceland	98
CHANGE	98
EGO	99
FREEDOM	102
JOY	106

Foreword

To the reader, the seeker, and now finder:

It is an honour to provide this Foreword for Alice's first publication, **Aliceland**. I have known Alice intimately, since my inception in fact, and perhaps even before that in previous lives. I am lucky and proud to call her Mami (mom in Czech) as well as my best friend.

Growing up, I witnessed my mom's special ability to connect with anyone and everyone in a very real, vulnerable, and meaningful manner. People of all walks of life gravitated to her like moths to a flame. Often referred to as "the life of the party," Alice had a bright and infectious energy that made people feel seen, understood, and good. Alice always put the needs and wants of others before her own. Despite this outward positivity and propensity to heal others, her life hasn't been without its challenges.

My earliest memories of her involve hospital settings due to her health issues, and later, her struggles with addictions and medically induced mental health injuries. It was not easy to bear witness to, and be impacted personally by, these challenges. Through my formalized training, I now understand many of Alice's shadows were an ineffective attempt to cope with pain and trauma.

Fortunately, in true stubborn Aries nature, Alice never gave up, no matter how many barriers were placed upon her path. In fact, anytime she was told "can't", "don't", or "shouldn't", by medical staff, family, or friends, Alice defiantly transmuted these sentiments into her motivation to overcome adversity. These efforts became the foundational bricks that paved her path to **Aliceland**.

Her strength, wisdom, and humbleness inspire those

who meet her and are afforded a glimpse into her life. Though her light has previously only shone on those whom she's met with face-to-face, it is my hope that this book will allow a broader reach, allowing thousands more to experience Alice, and embody Aliceland with their hearts.

Alice invites you, the reader, to examine your beliefs, patterns, attachments, and behaviours with an open mind as she chronicles the tools she discovered and applied on her journey into wellness. Mixing Western psychology with Eastern philosophies, Alice presents a simplified instructional, yet personalized, directive into wholeness and well-being. This book reads poetically. As you glide through artistically crafted metaphors, you will learn about the fundamental three Cs of Aliceland. Each presented concept is followed by gentle questioning and an opportunity to journal your responses and reflections, inspiring a deepened understanding of self. As one reads Alice's memoir, so too do they begin to capture their own.

It is no accident that you are reading this book. If you have ever felt life's pain, or believed yourself to be trapped in despair, have felt like life's circumstances are beyond your control, this book is for you. This is your chance, to make a choice, and create the change you are seeking.

Nicole Pesta

Daughter and Best Friend of Alice Pesta

Master's of Education in Counselling Psychology

Registered Provisional Psychologist

Nicolepesta.com

MY STORY

My name is Alice Pesta.

Living with a chronic illness for nearly forty-five years has helped me to create a unique technique for coping with stress and overcoming obstacles.

Let me tell you a story, my story.

I was born a healthy child in April, 1963 in the former Czechoslovakia. In 1974, my dreams came true when my mother allowed me to go to summer camp for the first time. The days were filled with activities, games, singing, and making new friends. I experienced the thrill of first love when, one evening, I was kissed by a boy. When I contracted the flu, there was no way I would tell anyone about it. That would be the end of my beautiful summer. I hid my high fevers and carried on in spite of my untreated strep throat.

But, Group B Streptococcus is ruthless. Without prompt treatment, it attacked my kidneys and eventually I was diagnosed with Glomerulonephritis IgA. The main purpose of the body's two kidneys is to filter the blood, clear all toxins, and send the excess moisture to the bladder. Kidneys are like a sieve. Imagine taking a sharp pencil and making little holes in the sieve. That is what this virus does. It is a slow process that can take many months or a few years for the kidneys to be destroyed. After camp, I ended up in the hospital for a period of two and a half months. While the initial attack was stopped, the damage done would eventually result in my kidneys failing.

In 1980, our family escaped the communist regime in a search for freedom and basic human rights. With a vision for a better tomorrow, my parents packed up the car with basic necessities, my brother Michal and me, and off we went for a holiday that would change our lives forever.

Fearful that we would be refused entry to Austria and sent back to face the worst possible consequences which could involve jail or manual labour for my parents, we were eventually permitted to cross the border. We spent the next year as refugees in a small Austrian village while our application for immigration to Canada was processed. I was able to make some money as a musician while my parents worked hard to learn English and at odd jobs here and there.

Finally, on April 30, 1981, eleven days after my eighteenth birthday, we flew to Canada. It was an incredible adventure for a young adult, imagining the vast opportunities that would open in the near future when we landed on the ground of our new homeland.

I enrolled at the University of Calgary and Michal continued high school. My father was hired by Mount Royal College where he taught physics for the next thirty years until his retirement. My mother also secured a wonderful job as an accountant in a collection agency.

By age twenty-seven, I was happily married to a loving man, Lou Pesta. We had two great children, Domenic and Nicole. Running a business with my husband, I had little time to worry about myself. We lived a healthy and active lifestyle. At home, I was always upbeat, laughing, singing and dancing in the kitchen while cooking and thoroughly enjoying my life. I saw a specialist once a year to keep track of my health and the productivity of my kidneys.

One day, feeling exhausted, I decided to leave work early to go home and rest. When I woke, I was in the hospital connected to a dialysis machine. I saw my blood being pumped out of my body to be artificially cleaned by chemicals. This was quite a shock. I had truly believed that I still had a few years to go before I would need any treatment. But, kidney disease is known as the silent destroyer and it can sneak up on you.

Although requiring attendances at Foothills Hospital three

times a week for around six hours at a time, I soon felt better.

After a few months on hemodialysis, I was able to change to peritoneal dialysis, which is not only easier on the body but also home-based. Peritoneal dialysis cleans the blood through a process of osmosis within one's own body cavity. This requires the surgical insertion of a connecting tube to allow for dialysis fluid exchanges to take place. For the next two years, I needed fluid exchanges four to six times a day. This required either being at home or at a very sterile location. Always looking at the bright side, I kept active in the community, went back to work, took care of our children, continued in sports and travelled as much as possible. Still, with this type of dialysis, each day always revolves around the scheduled exchanges and the constant risk of infection. The ideal solution to kidney failure is a transplant.

My mother, brother, and husband were all ruled out as suitable living donors and I was placed on the cadaver wait list. The waiting time for a cadaver kidney transplant at that time was three to five years (presently nine to eleven years).

Happily, in March of 1991, in the middle of the night, I received the best phone call of my life. It was a doctor from the Foothills Hospital. "Mrs. Pesta, WE HAVE A KIDNEY FOR YOU!" The emotion of happiness and love for the whole world that I felt then is impossible to capture in words.

On March 25, 1991, I received a new kidney which I lovingly named Lucy.

My body took some time to get used to the immuno-suppressants. I paid numerous visits to the hospital with bladder infections and migraines and to stay hydrated. Becoming a frequent patient, it seemed as if one room was reserved just for me. In addition, I underwent several more surgeries, including the removal of my native right kidney along with one of my ribs, having a tumour removed from the right breast, and later gallbladder surgery.

It is almost impossible to describe the improvement to the quality of my life once the medication doses were properly balanced and my body adopted the new organ. With the only demand being the twice-daily ingestion of anti-rejection drugs, my life returned to normal for a span of nearly twenty years. I marvelled at how wonderful our bodies are, even though we take them for granted. They are always serving us, allowing us to enjoy our lives and fulfill our dreams and hopes.

The year 2011 brought an abrupt change to my fabulous life. While golfing in Phoenix on one particularly windy day, I contracted a wind-borne virus called "valley fever." It hit me hard and my body landed again in the care of the staff at the Foothills Hospital, this time for nearly four months. What started as an inconvenient discomfort of cramping soon turned to vomiting, exhaustion, and dehydration. My legs swelled to the size of an elephant's, resulting in me requiring a wheelchair. In addition to the strongest drugs to fight the infection, I required numerous blood transfusions. Darkness overwhelmed me. Life lost its beauty and I found no reason to take the next breath. Without knowing what the next moment could bring, I continued living in pain, sadness, loneliness, and despair.

To make matters worse, through human error, Lucy—my baby, the donated kidney—showed signs of rejection. Trying to save her and going to extreme efforts to keep my blood clean were leading to a sad end. Death was in my thoughts and constantly fed me her stories of a painful end to my existence.

Although the infection was eventually defeated, Lucy suffered serious damage and its function started to decline.

By March of 2014, exhausted, I surrendered to the inevitable. Our son Domenic drove me back to the hospital to get help. Instead of being thankful to have this opportunity to continue my life, I was full of hate, anger, and blame. The clock was ticking, the moon was waxing and waning, doing her job, and life was passing me by.

To shake things up a bit more, in May 2014, we downsized from an acreage property to a downtown condominium. The move seemed to make sense as both of our children were living on their own and I was spending most of the winters in Phoenix, Arizona with Lou joining me for weeks at a time leaving the acreage home empty and vulnerable to the harsh Canadian winters. The move resulted in my exchanging peaceful nature and wildlife for a jungle full of concrete and very noisy gasoline-fed animals. The buses, cars, motorcycles, and other motorized vehicles constantly reminded me that I was not in Kansas anymore. Sleeping became a luxury, my mind was driving me crazy with the most negative, destructive, and self-defeating thoughts, driving me to the point of insanity. Lonely, depressed, filled with hate, smoking pot, and taking pain medication, I was just a shadow of the Alice I was, who had never known the word "problem."

In the past, I took challenges in life as a learning lesson to slow down, find a new way to continue living fully under circumstances presented at that time. During difficult times, after a few days of sorrows, I would soon find a way out of darkness through music, dance or cooking. With two young children, it was very important for me to create a happy harmonious home, which usually helped tremendously to lighten the weight I carried inside. Now, however, I had a hard time coping.

Temporarily crammed into a small downtown condominium apartment while we waited for our bigger condominium unit to free up, one of the bedrooms was completely filled with boxes of dialysis fluid, I was back on peritoneal dialysis. Progress had, however, been made over the twenty-five years since I had last needed this assistance in cleaning my blood. Now, I had a machine to assist with the fluid exchanges which took place while I slept. The machine was far from perfect and many times we were woken in the middle of the night with an alarm alerting us to a kink in one of the lines blocking the flow of fluid. I named my machine Cecilia, as she was "breaking my heart and shaking my confidence daily." Anxiety and phobias took over. I was unable to leave the apartment or speak to another person.

Sitting or lying down, staring at the ceiling, waiting for death to come and take me was my daily program. Then, at the end of February of 2015, we finally moved to our bigger condominium, just in the nick of time for the next transplant.

My wonderful husband Lou could not stand my suffering. After our daughter was ruled out as a suitable donor, Lou decided to donate one of his kidneys to a third party in the hope of securing a live donor organ in exchange for me. This is called a "chain organ exchange" and can at times involve up to eight or more people across Canada. Married for over thirty years, he had never seen me at such a low point, with no spark or any sign of life within me. His rationale was that since I already had his love and true heart, adding the gift of a kidney would make us even more complete.

On March 25, 2015, exactly twenty-four years to the day after my first transplant surgery, a new baby kidney joined Lucy. I decided to name the newcomer Julie. Unfortunately, the kidney did not do as well as the first one. Whether it was as a result of problems during surgery (although there were difficulties, I was told that I probably didn't want to know the details) or poor matching, Julie struggled from the outset. Performing at less than 30% of capacity at best and often straying below 20% she is still working well enough to permit me to stay off dialysis for now, but the long-term prospects are limited.

As a result of these problems, the new kidney initially failed to bring me happiness. I was still the same half-person, minus Cecilia the dialysis machine, and my negative thoughts and bad habits continued. I was fortunate to have a helper assist with my recovery at home. Liduska is an incredibly patient young lady who made sure that I ate and, while giving me space, was always by my side to help with my struggles. After six months, when not much had changed and I was sinking deeper into depression, refusing to speak or acknowledge reality, my kidney doctor recommended that I see a psychiatrist. I did and within five minutes was diagnosed as bipolar, and a very powerful antipsychotic was prescribed for me. And that was when I took matters into my own hands.

With a sense of responsibility and gratitude for Lou's gift, I knew that I had no excuse to delay getting better. I had proven to myself earlier that year that when I decide to make a change, I can. On Victoria Day, I quit smoking after thirty years. Although not a heavy smoker, I still had a daily habit that was stinking up this beautiful planet and destroying my already ailing body. Other positive steps which I will describe in more detail later quickly followed.

Today, once again, I feel free and am travelling the world helping people find the key to happiness and joy through Aliceland. The land of joy, peace, and serenity.

Aliceland is a program promoting love, faith, and integrity

to help each individual find the impulse within and RECOGNIZE the path to healthy living.

Growing up in the sixties and seventies without a television, my mother and dad were avid readers and I was blessed with many fairytales read to me until I learned to read. I would read every book offered in the library, many more than once. My mom would punish me by banning the books, which I would then hide in the house and with the use of a flashlight read secretly under the blanket until the wee hours of the morning in order not to be seen by a neighbour who would incriminate me to my mother. One of my favorite memories was of reading Alice in Wonderland. With this book, I could identify with and believe in anything I was experiencing in the environment from a very young age. And, I still do today.

Between my thirties and forties, I truly believed that we lived in LALA-LAND. My husband and I worked hard and our lives flowed marvelously with constant moving from one house to another, driving kids to various events, and being involved in our community and politics from the municipal to the federal level. After the "Velvet Revolution" in former Czechoslovakia, we went international when Lou was appointed as the "Honorary Consul of Czechoslovakia for the Province of Alberta and Saskatchewan." This position opened a new door and we were truly living in LALA-LAND. Young, full of positive energy, and trying to make the world a better place all around us.

In the fall of 2016, we were vacationing in Maui while working on a concept of how to share my miraculous change of life. From the darkest possible tsunami, hurricane, and war-like circumstances, to the light lifting me to a state of being impossible to describe. Through pure determination to find the Truth and later the Love for the Truth, the realization that it is I who creates my world. ALICELAND was born. Listening to the vibrations, Aliceland started to create a map to the door which opens the secret hidden within us. That realization and the power of the noun "LOVE" allowed me to decipher and manifest secrets which were previously unknown and hidden to me throughout my entire life.

THOUGHT

"Thought is constantly creating problems and then trying to solve them. But, as it tries to solve them it makes it worse because it doesn't notice that it's creating them. And the more it thinks the more problem it creates."

David Bohm

WHO IS THINKING?

When thought only reaches the first layer of the question, it has no ability to reach the seed of knowing and how to feed its needs to allow it to grow into fruition to reveal the TRUTH.

New daily experiences may expand our consciousness if we allow it. Sometimes, life will force us to redirect, readjust, and reform our field of vision and our beliefs to create harmony in our lives. It is important for the person to feel safe, otherwise inner conflict will bring discomfort and insecurities.

The mind can only work in the field of its consciousness to create an image for the brain to understand the message. Constant thinking and decisions based on false beliefs block the crossing of the bridge to the truth and reality. We are creatures seeking pleasure and fearing pain, trying to avoid it at any cost. To feel safe, we are willing to look the other way to ease the discomfort rather than face the truth. The mind will create its own reality to find a satisfactory solution. This pattern creates illusion and denies the truth.

Humans are like trees built from a little seed eventually spreading roots and growing a trunk and branches. To find a solution to any problem, we only prune the branches of the tree. In other words, rather than investigating the root of the conflict, which is within us, we only deal with the external issues. As we suffer, we only point fingers at others. Finding excuses, we blame the circumstance, or the other party, be it our partner, boss or a clerk at the grocery store. This pattern increases the belief of our identity as a victim.

This conclusion is based on a lie. We need to recognize that only we hold the power of our emotions and feelings and are always in control. We do not always have a choice as to whom we deal with or the situations we get in to, however, we always have the power to choose how we react or respond. When one chooses to react, he or she is repeating the same pattern out of habit which has been learned over time from experience. To respond, one looks at each circumstance as a new experience and treats it as such. Each response comes from the heart, not from the mind. To learn how to voice and hold our boundaries is the start of our safety and peace of being.

The healthy approach to each conflict is to ask the self if our perception of the situation is true. Getting to the root of the problem will allow us to recognize that it is I who holds the power to accept or reject what I am facing. If it is not true, then I can adjust my perception of the situation. If it is true, yet I am not in control of the environment, it is wiser to accept things as they are and go on with life. There are moments in our lives when it is wiser to swallow our pride, say "thank you," and leave.

Blaming others and playing the victim, calling friends and complaining is like trying to fix a broken leg with a band-aid. Reinforcement of our view of our story will thicken the shadows and prevent the revelation of the truth. It is necessary to allow one to see the whole picture, not just a fragment of any situation or problem, to allow the field of thinking to expand and find the best solution.

Denying the truth creates a conflict in the brain, and the same pattern repeats itself continually, re-activating the same thinking process. The ego needs to reassure itself of its existence, thus constantly digs in the past, trying to rewrite history or dreams of a future and then believes the imagined story and enforces it upon others. Activating the mind with a constant thought and constructing a false solution instead of adjusting the thought, the ego adjusts the facts. This is a habitual pattern created throughout civilization. The only solution to this error is to recognize the habitual pattern and eliminate it with conscious awareness.

Because the thought can only get as deep and extensive as the consciousness will allow it, we need to release the beliefs limiting the expansion of the mind. Through meditation and stillness, the realm of seeing the reality will clear the perception, eliminating psychological suffering.

The false belief then becomes transparent, allowing the mind to expand in consciousness. The individual is then able to understand and focus on the next step and realize how to adjust life, create harmony and acceptance. As the mind concentrate on one thought only, the energy and vibration of the perception changes.

Each day, each moment be happy and look forward to the possibility of living a happier life.

It is only a thought that creates a difficult knot, causing suffering. Rather than over-thinking the situation or the emotion, try to distance yourself from the situation. Go for a walk outside in nature, watch a movie, or start singing or dancing. If you chant, do chanting or read a book. To attain freedom from despair and sleepless nights one must cut the root of the disease, just like our hero in the Greek mythical poem of the Gordian knot. Once a poor peasant named Gordus became king of Phrygia. He dedicated his wagon to the greatest god, Zeus, for helping him. The pole of the wagon was tightened with a special knot. It was foretold that the man who could loosen that knot would become the ruler of Asia. Many tried but failed. Then, Alexander the Great came to the city and very simply cut the knot with one strike of his sword; he then went to conquer Asia. The lesson for us is that sometimes when we have a problem, we need to take decisive action.

Make a clean break—detach—and realize that we are in control of how to respond to any thought. Whether we choose to believe it or not, it is we who hold the power to change our lives in an instant.

Some thoughts are light and pretty like the clouds, yet sometimes we get hit by a hailstorm that freezes us solid and the circus of painful emotion repeats again and again.

Some thoughts make us happy and others make us miserable.

Have you ever questioned your thoughts?

Where does the thought come from?

Is the thought true?

How does the thought affect my being?

Can I control my next thought? Or, better yet, can I just observe it and let it go by like a cloud and allow the sky to clear?

A thought is one of the most powerful energies; it can kill or manifest a miracle. A thought can create a whole story in our head built from memories and images (experienced, heard or read, seen, felt, etc.) stored in the brain.

In the fall of 2014, I hit rock bottom, sleeping less than a couple of hours a night, hooked to a dialysis machine every night for eight hours, houseless, living on one of the busiest corners of downtown Calgary in a very small cramped apartment. We didn't unpack most boxes since this was a temporary residence, and as a result, I lived in a labyrinth of chaos. To magnify my misery, construction started across the street on an approximately thirty-storey building. Every day before 6:00 am, the pounding and thumping started and continued for twelve or more hours. I was used to living in a forest where the only noise was an odd crow or a coyote howling at night.

The most used words and my daily mantra were "I hate my life." The word HATE was in every sentence, every thought, every breath. Sometimes, I used much stronger language.

There was no use in speaking about the situation with anyone. To think, to rationalize, to plead, or use any other method to break the darkness I was living in I would have to first recognize the root of the problem and I was in absolute denial of the whole situation. I was falling deeper and deeper into despair and believed that I was worthless and that I should not be breathing the oxygen, eating the food, or continuing living.

The whispers from my childhood (I grew up in the sixties and seventies in the former Czechoslovakia) were threatening me: "Those who do not work should not eat." "Those who do not work should be in prison." I lost my identity and spent hours just staring at the ceiling, slowly dying inside. The way I saw myself became the mirror of how I saw the world and my surroundings. There was no light anywhere; only darkness, dim and getting darker, darker.

The break came when I discovered meditation and affirmations. At first I didn't even know what those two words meant, but slowly I stuck to the program and found some healing guided meditations I chose from the countless light workers I discovered on Social Media.

Lightworkers are, by definition, sensitive. They're receptive to the energies in any room they walk into. They're attuned to other people's moods and feelings and to environmental factors such as chemicals, pollution, or noise. They're conscious of the presence of angels.

"And, they're also sensitive to other people's opinions. This sensitivity is both a gift and a lifesaving instinct. You see, your overall personality remains fairly constant throughout lifetimes. Once a lightworker, always a lightworker. Remember: You already are a spiritual teacher and healer. You were born one, and you've been practicing your art for lifetimes."

Doreen Virtue,
Lightworker

There were many choices, different approaches, and I was learning how to let go, to surrender, and to know myself.

My mornings were spent listening to affirmations, sometimes hours at a time. I wanted a new life. I did not want to hate myself and life anymore. I wanted that happy, fun, life-loving ALICE back and I was willing to go through the challenges ahead of me, whether they were big or small. I was determined and knew this was my last chance to survive.

The first and the most powerful decision I made was to replace the word HATE with the word LOVE. Slowly, black was not as black and there were sunny days here and there. Focused on the positive side of things, I kept an eagle eye on my thinking patterns. As soon as the hating started, I sat down, wrote down what had caused the shift and followed my pattern of thinking backwards until I could recognize the root of misconception and misunderstanding of the truth.

Sticking to the principles and being lovingly tough with the mind slowly cured the negative patterns of judging and comparing. The mind loves to constantly play tricks on us just to see if we are paying attention. If you catch yourself back in hot water, make a game of it and it will become fun. You may start laughing at yourself and find a doorway to many more great things and creative solutions on how to quickly recognize the possible trouble.

When I redirected my thoughts, I redirected my life, improving my health.

Recognizing the CHANCE to use the power within to face the suffering helped me rebuild and claim myself back. Today, I look forward to each new day and learning new things I could not even have dreamt about. The opportunities are as vast as an open ocean. I look forward to every day and seeing what the Universe has to offer. Discovering who we are and allowing ourselves to expand are the most exciting gifts we are all offered through our lifetime.

Stick to the daily routine of meditation and affirmation. Keep a diary or a journal. Be mindful of each thought and word you are creating. You are the creator of the change that is always within you and the world is ready to have you and love you. Be kind and loving to yourself, smile or simply laugh at the mistakes you think you make, they really are only stepping stones and important lessons and part of the growth and learning process.

How high have you set your goal? Now, let's go and get it. The Universe offers unlimited opportunities. In ALICELAND, we will take it one step at a time to help you reach the sky and then go beyond.

The Three Cs of Aliceland

Aliceland is a state of mind, a resolve not to submit but rather to flourish in the face of challenges that life will inevitably present to all of us during our lifetimes.

The first C is for CHANCE

Challenges are presented to us every day. Some small and some larger. Health challenges come less often but sooner or later they will present themselves to all of us.

The first step is not to submit and allow the challenge to take over and govern the rest of our lives. Every chance and challenge is an opportunity as well. Our body may be broken, but our minds can flourish in the face of any obstacle. Recognize the chance to improve your state of mind, your resilience, in the face of any challenge.

The second C is for CHOICE

Every challenge will present optional responses. Do not allow anyone, including doctors, to force you into what they perceive to be the best course of action for you. Question everything. Remember that ultimately the choice is always yours. Choices will always exist for you to take the path which is the most or the least travelled. Which path is easy and which is difficult? Which path will give you the most satisfaction? Become aware of all the choices available to you.

The last C is for CHANGE

Once you choose the right path, you must become absolutely determined, even ruthless, to complete the journey. Do not lose sight of your destination. If it means that you will need to give up your friends and even distance yourself from family, if that's what it takes to eliminate forces that would distract you from your end, then do it. Be disciplined. If you maintain your focus, then you will reach your goal. ***Aliceland*** is possible.

The First C of Aliceland

CHANCE

RECOGNIZE

BE WISE

BELIEVE

CHANCE

RECOGNIZE

CHAPTER 1

Living day by day, week by week, year by year, I, along with everyone else, am conditioned by the environment into which I was born.

We are born free, without conditions, habits, patterns, or addictions. We do not have cravings, likes, or dislikes. All we need is food, warmth, and most of all LOVE. We are free of judgment, anger, hate, or attachments. Our mind is empty and our brain is healthy without any damage.

A newborn sees the world without any perception. Perception is something we learn through our experience of the world. Little babies may hear sounds we are immune or deaf to.

A young baby has no fear other than the fear of falling and a fear of loud noises. All the other fears are either learned or superimposed on us through stories of the elders, culture, or negative experiences. Sometimes, movies or books we read can influence our view and perception of what we see or believe and what we are afraid of.

As soon as we are out of the womb, we are numbered, labelled, and individualized. Depending on where we are born and what our parents believe we are given a name immediately after birth. A Christian child may be baptized, a Jew circumcised, a Hindu or Muslim's head shaved, somewhere else ears are pierced, and so on.

My first few years were influenced by my parents, family members, and the environment where I was learning basic human interaction. Always judged by my parents, family, and others who tried to determine whether I resembled this or that and from their perception labelling me according to whose traits I would inherit, was part of the process. Later, my behaviour and choices were guided and influenced by the people closest to me and as soon I began learning to speak, I repeated the words and the patterns of thought. This kind of conditioning and superimposition on a child from early development damages its ability to progress naturally. Just like in nature, when a flower or a tree is in its perfect environment nurtured by the sun, rain and enough space to grow it will produce the sweetest fruit, the same can be said with human beings. Those who are raised in a society supporting children to grow and pursue their talents or interests flourish. Those that are raised in circumstances where their every move is dictated and restricted will be limited in their natural thinking and development, often causing anxieties, misbehavior or apathy in the future.

Moulding me to conform to say what is acceptable, to think and do the same as the whole nation resulted for me in a slow and painful process of growing up..

Generally, I liked to please my parents in order to be praised and possibly rewarded. A lot of early learning is called latent learning. Even though it is not obvious at once, children mirror the behaviour of the parents as they grow. Whether it is body language or an emotional response to certain impulses language, attitudes, beliefs, and everything they live with day by day. At school, once again I behaved according to what was expected and required. Learning in a new way to think and act, I instantly wanted to learn everything from the teacher, because she knew best. One can suggest that I was being taught how to think and what to think and what to believe without ever questioning the studied material.

The curriculum was censored by the government dictating what was acceptable and what was not. Depending on the system, nationality, religion, skin colour, and other factors we live in, the traditions and history of the nation are strongly embedded into our beliefs thus separating us from others. Growing up in a communist Czechoslovakia, western cultures, countries, and people were compared and judged and we were taught negative opinions about them. This only enforced the ego and further separated us from others. We were never taught how to be mindful or what consciousness is. We were never taught to question our beliefs and views towards others and especially ourselves. The opinion about the Western countries and capitalism was strongly criticized. We were moulded to obey and serve and surrender to the government policies. If we chose to disagree openly with the system, the punishments were harsh. The more mature we were, the more severe the consequences were, including the torture and disappearance of the family members. Many great people simply disappeared, were jailed, teachers were let go. The communist ideology was forced into everyone's mind. Fear and mistrust suddenly entered the collective mind. Many individuals believed the false theory and were spying not only on their neighbours, colleagues but also on their immediate family members and anyone who would say, act or whisper a word against the communist party. It was a very dark period in Czechoslovakia.

Growing up, I too started to compare, label, and judge others, prejudice different cultures and everyone around me, yet deep inside my heart I knew that something was wrong with that. I started judging, doubting and belittling myself. With the lack of self-love and respect, I felt lost. I didn't know who I was or what was expected of me. Feeling separated and afraid, it would be frowned upon if I tried to stand out. I would punish myself for making the same mistake over and over again. That left me feeling worthless and in pain, both physical and mental. There were days when the emotions were unbearable. I would escape into television, food, alcohol, and later pain medications.

I escaped into books and music, to avoid dealing with the root of the problem of my feeling of separateness and the discomfort. I never thought of allowing myself to look deeper within.

I recognized the pattern as I got older and asked myself why. What is it that makes me believe that I cannot accept myself as I am at any moment and feel comfortable in the crowd?

I kept asking myself, "What separates me from the collective, making it difficult to fit in?"

Not only did I feel separate within the collective, but above all within myself. The EGO, the "me," was separate from the SELF, the Source. This conflict causes decisions to be made by the reason of the mind, which means the thought is often based on fear, rather than from the soul which would be coming from love. Always seeking to avoid pain and to find pleasure results in an internal struggle which causes unnecessary suffering.

By my early twenties, I had my life all planned out. Graduate University, find a partner, marry, have children, buy a house, and go to work. I would need adequate income to be able to pay for the mortgage, credit cards, children, groceries, cars, holidays, and everything else I wanted or needed. I was conditioned and my beliefs were solid, my will was strong to fill the desire to have all these luxuries and necessities. My desires forced me to often push myself to work beyond my body's healthy capacity, without listening to my body telling me that I was tired and should rest. Young and full of visions, I thought my body was invincible. Many of my friends have the same belief and hold onto a job which is secure but not always fulfilling or satisfying their heart. Some feel trapped, unappreciated and would love to move on. But, fear of the unknown stops them from such a bold step, and they suffer both mentally and physically.

People think the same thoughts, follow the same patterns, consume the same food they grew up with, dress similarly to everyone else in order to assimilate with the collective, to fit in and feel a sense of belonging. Watching the same or similar television programs, listening to the radio, watching news broadcasts, and following the media, in general, tends to increase the fear we already hold within and threatens our feelings of safety and wellbeing.

Most of us work hard at finding happiness. Billions of dollars are spent on advertising.

Every few minutes of every year, a new idea is introduced into one of the senses. Whether it is visual or the ones we hear on the radio and in the media. These messages are created slyly to sell you things you do not need, buy more rather than look for quality, and make you believe that with their products you will be thinner, prettier, smarter, cool, or just plain happy. Images of loving couples, great holidays, ecstatic children are featured.

Watching all these images activates the mind's instant desire to collect material objects and things. This is promised to result in "happiness" which we are always seeking to fulfill. Unfortunately, our desire for instant gratification is satisfied only temporarily. After a while, the newness evaporates and the feeling of something missing in life, a feeling of unhappiness, returns, bringing us back to despair and suffering. But, after only a short time, the pattern repeats and we once again search for something else to fulfill our new desire to complete us, truly believing that this time it will be forever.

Some of us make unhealthy choices to temporarily heal the inner hunger, pain or emptiness with sugar, excessive eating, alcohol, drugs, sex, overspending, gambling, and participating in various dangerous sports or activities that produce adrenaline highs. The choices are endless and in today's consumer market anything can be delivered to your door; sometimes within hours. This may prove disastrous. Many people are in debt with overwhelming payments and feel trapped. Fear, panic, and anxiety creep into their daily lives and stress builds up, forcing many to make drastic changes that cause unnecessary suffering. Unfortunately, shopaholics in today's culture are not only enabled but encouraged to shop online with constant pop-up ads.

Keeping ourselves busy with everyday chores and responsibilities, we often forget to take care of our bodies. Some of us avoid annual check-ups for various reasons. But, this is not the way to go as the consequences can be life-changing.

One of my friends finally decided to go for the dreaded annual physical after skipping several years. Feeling healthy with just a few aches or pains and an occasional cold or sniffle gave her a false sense of security. She was fooling herself that the importance of a regular check-up is just a myth. After all the blood work and some of the usual tests, she went back to the doctor to discuss the results. She learned that her tests revealed some abnormalities. It turned out that she had, in fact, contracted a disease which needed immediate treatment, medications, and possible surgery.

Her life changed abruptly. Her future suddenly looked very different than planned. A complete cure is possible, but it is not clear how long the healing will take or if it will succeed. Her life will never be the same.

These shocking trials happen every day, everywhere, and to many of us. When we are young, we believe that we are invincible and will live forever. Only some of us learn to eventually accept our own mortality or even contemplate it.

Life is like a game that must be played. We all have many chances every day to choose the right moves. Each choice brings us closer to the next move, each moment requires a decision about what to do next to find security and avoid pain and suffering. Because we are too busy doing things, living life, we have little time to ever consider that there are challenges which could halt the flow of daily activities and bring the flow of life to an abrupt stop.

CHAPTER 2

My day came on November 9th, 2015. After struggling with the reality of the poor transplant result and keeping my sanity and life together by a thread, my kidney doctor recommended a psychiatrist at the same facility. The psychiatrist listened to my struggles and asked me several questions. Answering honestly, I trusted the doctor to accurately diagnose the cause of my crippling bouts of depression. However, within a span of a few minutes, the doctor determined that I suffered from a severe bipolar disorder and prescribed a high dose of an extremely strong antipsychotic.

I had previously been prescribed medications affecting my brain and thinking and behaviour. While taking such medication, my personality and behaviour gradually changed and there were times when my actions and conduct were unpredictable. Bouts of anger, turning to fury would come and go unpredictably and life became that of a roller-coaster. After studying the side effects and comparing my suffering to other patients who were going through the same issues, and weighing the pluses and minuses, I decided that I had no other choice but to eliminate the medication. Not only did I stop using the meditation causing my uncontrolled behaviour, but I also decided to stop seeing the specialist.

A chronic disease may be complicated since many of us have been ill since early childhood and we were taught to listen to authority. Sadly, many of us never gained control and others were making our major life decisions. In my opinion, learned from past experiences, doctors are also only human and often misdiagnose a patient. I have always assumed that the combination of patient, doctor, and the pharmacist was a team where we all worked TOGETHER to help the patient heal as fast as possible. Best results are achieved when the patient is willing and able to take responsibility for his/her own well-being seriously.

Once again, I was standing at a crossroads. I was determined not to allow someone else to make the decision about where my next road would take me. I had to choose to go left (take the medication) or right (refuse to follow the diagnoses), based on which would be least likely to return me to pain medication or alcohol and addicted television watching. My prior decision in a similar situation resulted in further suffering.

I knew by instinct that there must be another solution. If I could only go inside and through the silence and stillness to hear the voice of my soul. Maybe then I could find the key to the Gate of Freedom and fully connect to the Source.

Should I continue to struggle, or should I take the chemical way out? Our daughter, Nicole, said to me a few profound words that have stuck with me to this day:

"THE CHOICE IS ALWAYS YOURS."

These words inspired me to face the demons, addiction, patterns, and illusions, and to follow through each step to find my real Self.

I had to make the right choice.

I was struggling.

This was a "Fundamental Decision."

My future depended on it. Somewhere inside, deep within, was a little voice, a little quiver, a vibration saying...this is it...I must change!!!! My whole body/mind felt this energy vibrating through my spine into the neck and my brain was just tingling with fear, doubt, despair. It was as though some other power within was warning, whispering ... be careful...

I asked myself...who am I????

Whose voice was I hearing pleading to be rescued?

Who is this voice I hear trapped in the depth inside of me held by my deeply wounded and threatened Ego?

Looking into the mirror, there was an image, but an image of whom? A stranger looked into my eyes and I was longing to have myself back again. I was frightened. I was afraid of my ghost self—the Ego. There was a monster in the mirror and my mind was addicted to it. It was its creation.

Was it the Ego's mind that frightened me, or was it the other way around? Was it the mind that created the Ego? I started screaming and fell to the floor in agony, crying and howling like a wounded animal about to die.

Where was the confident, happy positive being I remembered from the past?

Was she real?

Who is this person I know nothing of? I want to have myself back again.

I knew one journey of my life was ending. A new journey was just beginning. This is what have I learned.
When I reached the bottom, I had no choice but to sit down and get serious if I wanted to find peace and happiness. I only wanted to wake up from this treacherous dream and be happy.

I wanted to wake up and look forward to what the days ahead of me had to offer.

There were some basic but important questions I needed to face and answer:

Who is it that directs my actions?

Who is it that accepts the order and then acts?

The patterns and habits dictating my life were like a program on a computer hard drive. Except the "computer" was my thoughts and my mind.

In early childhood, I was labelled a chronically ill patient. Accepting that label I perceived myself as a patient with a serious chronic disease. I was under doctors' supervision most of my life and slowly lost my identity. Craving to be loved and accepted, fearing upsetting the doctors and nurses and everybody around me, I believed that I was stuck here in this unhappy world in this unkind Universe forever until I die. Looking for an excuse and blaming the circumstances, pointing to others to avoid discovering the truth was the norm.

After the transplant, I felt as though each day brought a deeper feeling of emptiness, sadness, and exhaustion. These feelings increased the belief that only the medications could keep me alive, thereby keeping me from change. With the program, I was not capable of making any changes, in case I might delete all the previous files and programs and download a new one, eliminating the self-sabotaging patterns and the negative thoughts.

The conflict in my head triggered the brain to feel insecure, activating the mind to find a way to understand the problem. The mind would shift to an automatic thinking process and thoughts started to create stories, excuses, and answers to find a temporary sense of peace or happiness. In the past, I may have started watching television, with some tension in the body to take pain medications, etc. That pattern would repeat every time I felt any discomfort or unease within myself whether emotional or psychological.

In the last hundred years, human beings have become human doings. In the last twenty-some years with the convenience of online shopping, the society is leaning more and more towards consumerism. With the false belief that we need this or that to satisfy our desire and fill the emptiness many of us feel inside, we are forced to work more and do more. Mobile phones, new technology, new demands every day busy our mind constantly.

Credit cards are good helpers, but can quickly become the master and a tyrant. Overspending creates stress, which then changes how we perceive reality. An individual who is under duress because of a lack of funds and due payments each week or month lives in a world of fear and panic.

Answering the above questions, digging deeper, I could not remember the last time I had allowed myself to be without a thought, either blaming myself or judging myself, others, or situations. I could not remember a guilt-free or shame-free day in nature or in bed just watching a movie. A day where no thoughts of "should" or "must" would prevent me from being fully present.

My journey was just beginning, and I was eager to start to discover the new/old me.

I felt strong vibrations within my whole being. This was my CHANCE.

Questioning all my beliefs and the decisions that I was making based on the five senses became a habit and eventually my second nature. I observed what was happening out of the body and the reactions/responses within the body.

Slowly recognizing the pattern of the mind and the constant

thoughts flowing regardless of its content, it was as though a busy mouth commented on every possible impulse from either perception or sensation just to verify and ensure its existence.

Sitting quietly in stillness, I started practicing the being. There were moments when I could feel the mind sinking deeper, allowing the mind to rest if only for a glimpse. But, the body would start trembling and the thought came back, frantically trying to acknowledge its "reality."

SEIZE THE CHANCE!

This was a time of learning about myself. The question, who am I? And what am I made of? Suddenly, I found myself at the bookstore standing in front of books about astrology, the self-help section, and self-improvement.

My first book was *The Power of Now* from Eckhart Toole. I understood some of it, yet the deeper his thoughts went the more lost I became.

Recognizing what is important to me, I started digging deeper. YouTube became my best friend and my new virtual family was Luise Hay, with her incredibly kind and patient approach to the broken and almost dead inner child. Starting from scratch, I began to recognize that the deep pain of rejection and constant disapproval from my parents were the cause of the resulting unhappiness in my life filled with extremes. As soon as the pain would activate, my unconscious mind would go into overdrive and all decisions and actions were based on fear, resulting in destructive outcomes. Some of them were significantly fateful.

Meditating with numerous videos from Jason Stephenson, Michael Seally, and many others, I was learning from their stories and how they were coping with their transitions and transformation in awakening and broadening their minds and consciousness. Everyone who was honest would describe moments of misery, pain, and wet pillows of tears flowing like the avalanche of emotions, pain, and regrets. Blame, shame, anger, hate, and countless showers and screams of despair and anguish were followed by days of numbness, small deaths, and giving up on life altogether. Unable to be or do, I was just that matter which was breathed into and functioned like a robot. Food became tasteless, the eyes saw nothing, and things were just passing. There were countless hours of nothingness interspersed with sudden moments of extreme happiness and energies with loud music, dancing, singing; the me was not dead yet, but the I, The Higher Self, was reassuring me that I must keep on fighting. This energy came from the deepest being within when the mind and body were "dead" in any of the five senses.

Learning how I perceive the past and what impact it has on me now, each thought would be examined and, if persisting, I would write it down to understand the bottom of its reappearance. Soon enough, I knew the long "forgotten" memories, which were never forgotten. They were just buried deep in the unconscious mind. This was a process of learning how to become an observer and experience the memory of the wound through the eye of a witness.

When I perceived any situation, I was detached and allowed the emotions to flow through, yet was not affected by them. There was a feeling of two beings in one and I felt safe. This process took patience and lots of self-love and compassion. Not only for myself but those who were the cause of the pain and suffering that had caused the misshaping of the identity or shattered ego.

Living in the now was difficult to begin with, but got easier with diligent persistence and determination to heal and never repeat the experience of the horror that had brought me so close to craziness. I was escaping the horror and negative consequences of almost giving over my authority to the doctors and nurses and the staff in the pharmacy.

A secure and loving future was becoming a possibility and

bursts of encouragement would come from strangers, books, songs, and steadiness. I was learning to take things one day at a time, sometimes one breath at a time, and to perceive the world with a new eye.

Staying alive and happy was reinforced with daily affirmations not only in the morning, but anytime I felt the impulse of the pattern from the past. Dark thoughts were observed, never dismissed, and questioned so as to not allow them to become a reality of the mind and body. Recognizing the lies and accepting the truth would free me and the sun was shining longer, warmer, and healing became a daily pleasure. Just to sit and be still and silent became my favourite non-activity.

Answering and responding to all the questions honestly started to shape the next step I was ready to take.

I recognized that in the darkness there was an opportunity to contemplate the CHANCE to examine the difference in my perception of reality discovering the light of being. Only then could I make a CHOICE.

I would suggest that it is wise and necessary to understand the desire and be clear and honest with answers to the following question:

What do I want?

Take time and look at yourself from a higher perspective and recognize that we are all connected, not only with other human beings but with nature, animals, Gaia, and the whole Universe and beyond.

Inevitably, there comes a time in our life journey when we ask ourselves the additional simple question:

WHO AM I?

We are all taught to believe that we are either a man or a woman, mother, sister, daughter, and so on.

Then, we go further and start looking at our shape as being either tall or short, slim, or full-bodied, etc.

Some consider him or herself as more intelligent, introverted, compassionate, kind, lazy, funny, and millions of other abilities and characteristics.

People perceive status in attaining university degrees, having children, perfect bodies, a big house, or an expensive car.

We need to shed all the above-mentioned labels and investigate further, beyond the superficial form.

Who are we past these possessions?

Who is the I that is always there, never changing, always with me. The I who is not the personality, who is not the person who is that which has been and will be with me in me until the last day? When our lives and our image disappear right in front of our eyes, we have no choice but to find out what we are really made of.

This is called self-inquiry.

This gives us the CHANCE to realize who we truly are.

May I propose that you do not rush this process through quickly and carelessly as your future may be changing drastically and it is in your hands where fate will take you? Allow this new knowledge to sink in and keep on digging further to experience who you are. Sink in and be comfortable with the decisions you are making.

When we receive sudden unexpected information from a doctor, or an employee, or shocking news of the death of a loved one, or win a large amount of money or maybe receive an unexpected wedding proposal, any of which may drastically change our daily life and our identity, do not allow the mind to create a story and quickly believe it. Do not build your future on a false premise or an illusion. Recognize the bond of duty and the bond between thinking and doing. Changes are not possible without full control of the thought.

What is "Limitation?" Limitation is our belief in the illusion that has been superimposed on us for thousands of years. Recognizing, accepting, and lovingly transforming/expanding consciousness will allow us a deeper understanding of reality and to reach closer proximity to the Truth.

What is "possibility?" Possibility depends on how honest we are prepared to be; whether we are ready and willing to shed that which we thought and believed to be true and discard it as a dream and start living with an empty mind. In other words, we only use our minds while working or creating. But we are free of the constant dialogue or flow of thought or images we are addicted to not being aware of. This does not mean that we forget all practical memories, like how to get home or to drive a car and so on. All the experience through which we are able to continue to exist in this universe will stay with us, often lighter in their essence.

Waking up from a long deep sleep is a shocking and often painful experience. There are many ways to spend life chasing and following thoughts and desires. Often the outcome depends on who it is that is making the choice.

Who is thinking? The one thinking will be the one choosing. And the one who is thinking is the one who holds the control of the thought and mind and the desire. To recognize if we live in a pattern (ego) or if we realize we are the awareness (the higher self) will dictate the outcome of each thought.

Who is the knower? Once again, this depends on who is

thinking or if thought is required. Depending on whether the I (the higher self) or the body/mind make the decision to choose what the truth is, the result may be different. The body/mind desire is usually perceived on the object/subject pattern where the higher-self always sees the whole picture of the collective and the decision is made through selfless act for the best for all.

Who decides? Only two possibilities exist. If we live in an illusion and believe that our reality is form based on matter, then the body/mind will be the decision-making authority. Should we realize that we are awareness and guide our being, the decision will be based on pure absolute knowing.

As we realize who we are and remember the talents that we never pursued, we could feel the sudden urge to break free and do so. The gifts we are all born with will want to be manifested and we may break free from the controlling parents, teachers, and other possible authorities as we get older and realize our true nature.

Occasionally, a time comes when we manifest the seed of our creativity to benefit not only ourselves but also others, allowing us to live a life filled with love and compassion.

It seems that the mind is constantly working and trying to become somebody; comparing, judging, not trusting, shaming, etc.

The constant need for approval, reassurance, and acknowledgment that we are doing the right thing is the Ego crying out through our mind. Fear, anxiety, and the need to be accepted by others is what holds us back from making our dreams come true.

Find the patterns, habits, and false beliefs that have been and are constantly thrown at you and superimposed by society, the media, etc. Be conscious each moment and aware of your senses and feelings. Above all, observe each thought and ask who is thinking.

When the time comes to make the choice, ask yourself:

"Who is making the choice?"

Through meditation and expanding your consciousness, your true essence will awake. This is a process that may take many weeks or months or years, as you will recognize old habits, and patterns of thinking that are self-sabotaging your progress of self and preventing you from becoming realized.

Now that you are an authentic being and you have shed the attachments and the doing part which you believed and followed most of your life, sudden shifts and changes may start happening. A wave of simplicity and invisible help appears to be available for us to grab or follow. Embrace each moment with kindness, compassion, joy and caring.

Nature teaches us the beauty of life if we are willing to learn the lesson and align with the message. Just like the praying mantis stays for hours without a blink, knowing that her lunch will be served shortly. Let us too assume the position of knowing who we are and that what is ours will come to us with the grace and beauty of stillness and silence.

BE WISE

Each question you'll find an answer to leads to another question. Investigate each one carefully and quietly in meditative contemplations. Take time to learn how to search deeper within and ask yourself if the answer feels true to your being. Just because we have believed something for many years does not mean that it is true. Listen not only with your ears and other senses. Go deeper beyond the physical world of the mind and beyond the emotional garden to feel if what is said vibrates with you.

I once read:

"The problem with making assumptions is that we believe they are the truth. To assume what is or what we believe, we mislead our mind of what is truth and later take the situation and the outcome personally. The Ego reacts by sending emotional poison with the word. This creates a whole big drama for nothing."
THE FOUR AGREEMENTS BY DON MIGUEL RUIZ

Always keep in mind that you are only perceiving the world through your eyes, ears, or other senses and the information sent to the brain is a mirror image. The person then receives the message and creates their own reality. Be aware to realize the difference between what is real and what you think is real and only then allow the TRUTH to reveal itself.

Be diligent not to fall back into old patterns of thinking and beliefs.

This is the **CHANCE** to realize who you truly are.

Look at life through absolute reality and make an intelligent decision, based on truth, not assumptions or beliefs based on something you have read, or perceived. If it vibrates positively within you in every core of your being, then knowingly make the

CHOICE
to either
CHANGE
or not.

LEARN

Learn a new way of thinking.

When you look back at your upbringing, you will realize that many daily tasks that we now carry out automatically without a thought had to initially be learned; from crawling, to feeding, to dressing, etc. Start simply by walking and paying attention to everything involved in the process. Be present and aware. Slowly get to know who you are. Be kind to yourself and allow your being to unfold fully one breath at a time.

Writing was once a challenge for me, yet today I can write anything without a second thought. The trick is simple. Sit down, start writing, and let the story unfold itself word by word.

Thinking techniques were developed at school through education. Today in everyday life there is knowledge which is necessary for us to survive, such as remembering where we live or how to drive a car.

But, there is also knowledge we have learned and trust it to be true and yet it is based on wrong concepts and wrong assumptions.

This assumed knowledge we have inherited from our predecessors, based on a false perception, assuming it is so by default. This kind of thinking leads us to destructive decisions and therefore we always fall back into the trap and eventually fail at anything we are trying to accomplish, causing additional suffering.

Life experience teaches us that everything is not as it appears. May I suggest that you always take a moment and ask: Is it true?

Learn the difference between pain and suffering.

Pain is caused by physical discomforts, such as an injury or an underlying source of chronic pain. This pain also alters or may weaken over time, or be eliminated after taking medication.

Suffering, on the other hand, is purely mental anguish that continues to alter our perception of reality. It is only possible to eliminate this discomfort from our life when we learn and realize our true nature of who we are and the power of knowing.

Seek guidance from different sources and allow yourself to be a student once again.

Ask yourself, "Who am I?" often as your consciousness will expand and your identity with what you perceive will start to shift.

Accept the reality of not knowing and be OK with it. It is a rather freeing experience. Let life unfold in front of your eyes, letting the thoughts just pass like a cloud in the sky. With loving kindness, try to see the world through a new perspective without any assumptions or labels.

If certain thoughts keep coming back, write each one of them down and get to the root of them. Ask yourself, is it from the mind? Is it from the past or the future? Once you recognize the reason why it re-appears, you can face the possible attachment to a past memory and resolve it once and for all.

Take your time and do not hurry.

Each thought is important to allow yourself to feel light and free. This process might change the course of your life as you learn more about your Self.

When a thought becomes a word and the word turns to action, you are not a free man, as there will be a reaction. After all, you are what you think, therefore always ask yourself—who is thinking?

What is the concept of the thought?

Is the thought true, relevant, or is it just a distraction of the mind or the ego?

The addiction to a constant chatter inside your head with multitudes of thoughts can result in what is often labelled "Monkey Mind;" the jumping from branch to branch, from one thought to another, to distract the mind and prevent it from being aligned with its source.

If a thought comes from silence, from the stillness inside you, and feels supportive of who you are, then either accept the thought or let it go just like a wave on the surface of the ocean.

Be kind to yourself and make it a game, not a challenge. Learn to reveal more about yourself and learn how wonderful the vibration of knowing is. Suddenly, life will be like sailing a boat on a clear ocean with such peace and calmness within. And with that vibration, no matter what we face in our lives, we do not feel afraid or in conflict.

Treat yourself to a lot of rest and take good care of your body. You deserve it. Do not forget to thank the Universe, the Source, and yourself for every positive step towards your freedom, ending the slavery to the mind and the desires of the body one step at a time.

Alice Pesta

CHANCE WORKSHEET

RECOGNIZE WHAT YOUR ARE NOT

What are the habits and patterns you live in and follow unconsciously?

_____
_____
_____
_____

(i.e. When I feel pain/discomfort I get medicated)

Recognize the past conditioning

_____
_____
_____
_____

(i.e. obeying authority without questioning)

Question all your beliefs.

(i.e. I believe I am powerless without guidance from others)

Sit quietly.

WHO YOU THINK YOU ARE

When you look in the mirror, who do you see?

The image looking at you is exactly that—an IMAGE.

This image is a collection of your thoughts and emotions and memories throughout your lifetime. Your parents from birth have taught you all they knew, you then went to school, made friends. All these memories of love, fear, pain, anger, hurt, etc. are stored in that image inside your mind, which is stored inside your brain. It is always changing, always different. From this box of memories, all our thoughts come, repeating the same ones over and over, re-affirming and strengthening the prejudice of our identity.

Our mind creates the "me," the Ego, the image. The Ego is never constant and never fully satisfied, always desiring to be different and creating conflict in the brain as it resists change. When the ego feels threatened, it reinforces resistance and the refusal to see reality. The fear of its existence separates us from the Source. The Ego does not see the truth but perceives the image from memory, therefore, lives in an illusion.

This was the time I was learning about myself.

Recognizing what is important to me and naming it, writing it down, and reinforcing it by daily affirmation.

Learning how I perceive the past and seeing it as that past and letting go.

Questioning how I perceived the now and recognized the TRUTH.

Asking myself whether I could build a secure, loving future in the now, thus eliminating the future.

Learning and accepting that the future is just another illusion of the mind as Future does not exist and I have no control of what is beyond the now.

Inquire can I stay alive and happy with only myself?

These were the questions shaping the next step I would take.

I recognized that in the darkness there was an opportunity to grab the CHANCE and examine the difference in perception. Only then could I make a proper CHOICE.

It is wise and necessary to understand the desire and be clear and honest with answers to the next question.

What do I want?

_____

_____

_____

_____

(i.e. I want to be loved and accepted)

When any doubt comes from the mind (ego), ask who am I?

And ask who am I beyond these possessions and labels? Go deeper into the core of yourself.

Keep eliminating labels and possessions. Life will become lighter, less worrisome.

Allow yourself to see that you are the Universe.

Ask yourself: am I limiting myself in this decision or am I allowing space to expand into my full potential with room to grow?

_____
_____
_____

(i.e. I commit to stick to a new routine and grow without expectation)

What is my possibility right now at this moment?

_____
_____
_____

(i.e. I can try my best to walk ten thousand steps every day)

Who is thinking?

_____
_____
_____

(i.e. Is it my head or my heart thinking?)

Who is knowing?

_____
_____
_____

(i.e. Is it "me", the Ego with make-believe, or the Self with Truth?)

Who decides?

_____
_____
_____

(i.e. Is it the head or the heart—fear/love based decision?)

THE MIND

It is necessary to be aware of the origin of each thought and every decision we are about to make. As the thought gets processed by the brain, the reaction or response will be based on the information received from it. I have learned that my thoughts, and therefore thinking, were mostly based on lies and illusion, therefore I had seldom felt comfortable with the reality of the world I was growing up in. It took me a long time to recognize and adjust my perception. But, I would encourage everyone to take the time and allow the world to be seen as it truly is.

It is miraculous when the mind is in an absolute stillness and silence and the beauty of truth with the clarity and love penetrates through manifestation of creation, whether it is poetry, painting, architecture, dance, music and so on. It as if heaven is painting earth with golden dust of love.

"A QUIET MIND is all you need.

When the mind is quiet, we come to know ourselves as the pure witness.
We withdraw from the experience and stand apart in pure awareness
which is between and beyond the two".

Nisargadatta Maharaj

BE WHO YOU ARE

KNOW WHAT TO DO

HAVE WHAT YOU WANT

The Second C of Aliceland

CHOICE A

THE PILL

HONOUR

RELEASE

GRACE/BLESSINGS

CHOICE B

THE PILL

FEAR

SUFFERING

CHOICE

When the time comes, it is up to us to make the choice between taking the imaginary Red Pill or Blue Pill.

THE BLUE PILL

Continue living under the same beliefs, views, and perceptions that most of our friends, family, and coworkers live under now. Follow the same truth and teachings we were taught for the past hundreds and even thousands of years as they were passed from generation to generation without any question or doubt. Follow the same rules, the same programs, and the same thoughts you have been conditioned to and had superimposed upon you since your birth.

There is absolutely nothing wrong with that. You know exactly where you are going; the road has been paved for you. There will be obstacles with many possible solutions which are tried and tested and were followed by billions before you.

Most people today see themselves as a subject who needs to follow authority (object) that dictates or teaches us our next step. We base our beliefs on the past and make choices as separate beings (I or we, us) against them (the other). These decisions are made from a collective conscious mind which has been superimposed upon us for millions of years. Always feeling separate from the outside and then comparing it to the inside, we see only that which we are consciously capable of seeing within ourselves. This leads to a fragmented picture that misses the whole view from above.

This logic is based on duality thinking. The following is a simple example to help in understanding this concept. As we separate one part from the other, fragmenting the whole imaginary pie (the situation) into pieces, we can go further and break each piece a little more into the substance it was made of (the flour, eggs, butter and other ingredients measured and combined in baking the pie). And, if we want to search even further, we can put tiny pieces under a microscope and find a whole new world not visible to the naked eye. In the end, we will end up with billions of fragments of the pie, but the image of the pie will disappear altogether in the process. (This is sometimes referred to as not seeing the forest for the trees)

When we make decisions on an assumption and judge the situation from accumulated memories, we react in the same way as always. As I explained before, our brain is the storage of innumerable memories and experiences. To voice that which is inside the mind, we use symbols such as words, feelings, music, art, etc. From early existence, each of these experiences is perceived and locked in memory and we then assume and perceive each new day or situation the same.

But, not always are the choices and beliefs based on truth and reality. Imagine walking to work or school, taking the same route each day. We become blind to the constant changes, and instead assume that what is happening at this moment is the same as any other day, yet is it so absolute, or is it new?

We believe that things are as they are perceived as it gives us comfort. When we still the mind without any messages, there is a moment of serenity until a thought disturbs it. This happens so quickly that we hardly recognize it. Unless we are consciously aware, we will react. Feeding the thought strengthens the story and an illusion is created from the past scenario. In other words, if I am walking to work and someone bumps into me from behind I could get instantly angry. When I turn and recognize the person to be disabled, my anger dissipates, and the emotion turns to empathy or compassion.

When looking at each situation as good or bad, temperatures as cold or hot, or judge individuals constantly as either being beautiful or ugly, smart or stupid, sick or healthy, and distances as far or close etc., we feel separated from the wholeness. We apply the same concept when we look at ourselves judging our own looks, intelligence, weight, and mood, hardly seeing and accepting ourselves as we truly are—which is perfect. With the pain and suffering from the past, many of us believe that we are not good enough and nothing can ever change.

The world today is perceived through duality and everything is looked at as a subject and object. This gives individuals a false assumption that they are in control, often resulting in disappointments and suffering.

THE RED PILL

I, on the other hand, have chosen the Red Pill.

The life I lived as recently as 2015 cannot even come close to comparing to the life I am experiencing today. In the summer of 2015, I was broken, full of fear, unfocused, without control, without a plan or anything to look forward to. Life consisted of suffering, despair, pain, fear, anger, and tears. I just existed day to day, week to week in between doctor's visits, believing there was no way out from the dark abyss I held in my mind's perception.

Today, I see the world from a new perspective. Eliminating the mind's illusionary perception, there are no imaginary problems with anything I choose to do or accomplish. I am comfortable with the ability to recognize what is true now with absolute clarity. There are only lessons to learn from every moment of existence.

I continually experiment with new approaches and attitudes towards daily living from the moment I wake up and open my eyes until the moment I am ready to turn off the mind for a good night's sleep. Recognizing that I am not in control of a given situation or another person, I now realize that the only solution to anything is how I choose to respond. I consciously slow down and observe the flow of life exactly as it opens up in front of my eyes.

Realizing that I am responsible for everything that is happening to me was the most profound breakthrough past the veil of the illusion which was covering my eyes. Not allowing the mind to wander into the future or dig into the past, I recognized the insanity of the old patterns keeping me in the dark. As a result, conscious decisions from this new discovery always prevent me from falling back to the bottom of the ditch of ignorance. The truth is here and now.

It happened suddenly one day while I was meditating. I could feel and see the oneness; the whole being. There was peace and joy from within and around me and I could see the truth, the absolute reality. I was able to recognize that all is perfect and all is in order. Slowing down and connecting to my heart was the key that opened the door to the light. It was obvious to me that I was there, and yet I was not, I was in a dream. It was such a sweet beautiful pain-free dream of such beauty and love supported by loving compassion. This life-changing experience can only be felt and there are no adequate words to describe or explain it.

In trying to understand this sudden shift in myself, I started seeking through many spiritual and philosophical paths, trying to recreate this empowering experience of Grace. Instantly, I became a seeker of the TRUTH. On this pathless journey, I'm learning so much every day. My attitude turned to gratitude and at times I feel like the true *Alice in Wonderland*. I learned so many new and exciting concepts.

For example, did you know that our human mind is separated into two kinds of knowledge? Conceptual knowledge based on object—subject and non-conceptual knowledge based on accepting things as they are without preconditioned thinking and not separating them from the whole "pie," which had no beginning and no end. I could understand the Yin and Yang and the whole concept of this miracle.

    I have questioned everything that I thought was true in the past and started to observe everything from each new thought, to every slight body movement, emotion, and reaction. Like a hawk or eagle, I would guard each word and all body/mind sensations I was experiencing. Every time a conflict within the body/mind had risen, I would observe everything within myself as well as keep a scrupulous intensive awareness on what was happening around me. I made no judgment, no comparison, no assumption. This transformation took a while, but with practice, it slowly became natural for me to see myself as the space I was in. Suddenly, I was floating. The body was used as a vehicle of which I was the driver.

HONOR YOUR CHOICE

Take all the time. This is a slow and at times challenging and laborious process, if one chooses to label it. I decided that if I wanted to evolve, I must be fully present, aware and still within the Self to clarify every step. Think of it as a teething cycle involving lots of drooling, with tears of pain from yearning, sleepless nights, and fear of the unknown. The mind will try to return to the old conditioned behaviour and beliefs. As soon as one is not consciously aware of the HERE and NOW, the ego will take over, the mind will try many tricks to lure you back to the life of suffering. The body may not like to move and exercise, but you must stick to it. THAT, which feels and tastes like poison now, will be the sweetest ambrosia or immortal meal you have ever tasted. It is like the bear that braves receiving a few bee stings in stealing the yummy sweet nectar from a beehive. He knows that the sweetness of the fruits of his labour, honey, will take all of the discomfort away. The same desire to achieve peace and joy needs to be immense to give us the strength within to continue seeing the TRUTH and shedding all the predispositions and conditions superimposed on the human mind.

Our mind is conditioned just like Pavlov's dog. When the bell rang and the red light was lit, dogs were then given food. After a short while, the dogs reacted to the stimuli by salivating every time with or without food. Observe each conditional behaviour initiated from the five basic senses every time an impulse or stimuli of one or more of the senses occurs. For example, a commercial for pizza or ice cream will activate the mind which, in turn, will generate a craving which will automatically cause us to get up and walk to the fridge or pantry to get a snack. The very important word here is "automatically," proving that most of our activity, whether it is our thought or body, is conditioned and automated from past experiences and latent learning.

Did you know that it is now believed that beyond the five basic senses there are as many as twenty-one more? The sense of touch (somatic), for example, can further be divided into the senses of pressure, heat, and pain.

Keep on chiselling, perfecting, eliminating, or replacing every condition, every habit that has been taught, learned, and engraved into the mind and body. Question the thinking process and seek answers. Become a witness to your own patterns of thinking and reactions to emotions, situations, or relationships. It is said that you need to practice a thing 10,000 times or more to learn and perfect it. With determination, you can become an Olympic athlete, a pianist, or a tennis player, anything that you desire. On the other hand, it is much easier to develop and master bad habits such as binging, gambling, laziness, watching too much television, spending too much time on the computer and, of course, drug and alcohol abuse. Keep asking yourself what is real and what is the truth.

The process is not unlike the unravelling of the Christmas lights which got all tangled up into one giant knot when put away in a box last year. Starting from the end you go backwards to slowly untangle each length and knot. Focusing on the task, it gets easier and easier as you follow the cord. The same thing applies to the process of our thinking and behavior. Recognize honestly who you are, here and now. With no judgment and with no harsh thought. Be honest with questioning yourself when examining what is preventing you from attaining joy and happiness. Even though it seems like a slow and frustrating activity, if you persevere you will succeed in untangling the mysteries within the cluster of mess.

When the last knot is cleared, you dress the tree and the lights are turned on, the magnificent feeling of happiness, peace and accomplishment will flow through each cell. Your Self will become a radiant light enlightening the whole body. The whole Universe will shine through every spore. Your whole being will synchronize with the world and you will feel like you are back on your honeymoon. The fruit of the hard labor will bring tremendous peace and the realization of the beautiful miracle of being; a state of Nirvana. There will be a presence and the sense of being one with the Universe in a state of absolute Serenity.

Imagine that you are this tangled ball of Christmas light cord and focus on the cluster of thoughts, emotions and unnecessary despair. Ask yourself - where am I now? Let the enlightenment guide you to your inner spark and let it INLIGHTEN* the whole Universe. By connecting with the light you will discover your Higher Self. Once you recognize the true magnificence of who you truly are you will find inner stability and the most amazing feeling of peace, joy and happiness.

This incredible experience only happens when our mind is focused fully and completely on only one task and the brain is still. Our inner and outer body becomes one and we are in a so-called zone of being, yet the body is working. Or we may be sitting in a park and just looking at a flower or a tree and suddenly we sink into the Truth. It is an amazing experience to realize that we are not the doers.

Just like the ocean has many levels of different movements or energies, so is our mind layered with tens of thousands of thoughts. On the top of the ocean, there are many different waves moving and building up, smaller becoming bigger and faster and others slowing down and disappearing. The same thing happens in our mind; we have some thoughts that just move along steadily without much attention, other "tyrant" thoughts, as I call them, which can make us feel ever so small, and other explosive ones when we get angry or hurt and blame either the circumstances or another being. The Tyrant and Explosive thoughts can make one feel more pain and further separated from the Source.

To compare and to allow the mind to understand, let me use the waves of the ocean to explain the absurdity of our own self-sabotaging thoughts. Imagine a small wave is jumping on top of the ocean along with many others. As it is floating beside a bigger wave, would it ever compare itself?

And let's imagine the conversation: "Hello big wave, you must be wise and all knowing. Will we ever get to know the ocean? I have heard that the ocean is an incredible place to be." And the big wave would reply, "Oh, little wave, I have been chasing the ocean for a long time, but it may be far, far away."

And just like the waves feel separated from the ocean, we human beings feel separated from the Source which is veiled by our thoughts, making us unable to see the truth. When the mind is not present and is reliving the past or trying to figure out the future, it feels separated from the wholeness of reality and creates conflict and an uneasy feeling.

We need to realize that we are always aware and awareness itself is like the bottom of the ocean, always calm and still. Once we find this beautiful jewel within our body and learn to align together with the heart and mind and the outer environment, we too will stay calm and collected through the most difficult circumstances.

Understanding the seven CHAKRAS (teachings from the Indian Sanskrit roughly translated to wheel) allows one to attain stability and harmony with what is. When there is an impulse inside the chest, like a grip, the mind may perceive it either as fear, anxiety, pain, discomfort, or pleasure. Keeping a close observation on the thought pattern for at least seventeen seconds and considering the possibility that the mind is making an assumption and reaction from the body/mind based on the past, we can recognize and learn how to eliminate a lot of unnecessary pain and suffering. With practice and always paying attention and slowing down, soon it will become clear that many of our beliefs are not real but illusions. In a few weeks or maybe a month, we will feel suddenly in peace, comfortable, and happy anywhere, knowing we are in the HERE and NOW and supported by life itself.

"It is only when we silent the blaring sound of our daily existence that we finally hear the whisper of truth that life reveals to us as it stands knocking on the doorstep of our hearts."

K.T.Jong

HABITS

When I am sitting in a chair or lying on a couch, I try to understand what it is that brought me there. What are these knots in my body and in my mind through thought, which are at times quite painful, and hold me back from my desire to achieve happiness? These knots produce blockages within our bodies which can, in turn, affect our breathing, blood circulation, muscle movement, and overall health. Why am I here and not where I want to be? Just like unravelling the cord to find the light, I question my habits.

Human beings are very habitual creatures and perform countless chores or tasks daily without any thought. This is how we spend most of our time. There are good habits and bad habits. For instance, take the brushing of teeth, or the washing of your face. In the mirror, we see the image of ourselves. How many of us look in the mirror with a loving and approving attitude? Why do many of us dislike the image and judge, label, and disapprove of the self at all? This is a habit that we picked up early in our lives and just like in the *Snow White* fairytale, whenever there is a mirror on the wall the vast majority of us ask, "Mirror mirror on the wall...who is the fairest of them all?" Try to look in the mirror, pick up the toothbrush and with a mind focused on only brushing enjoy the two minutes of silence and stillness within the inner self and the task of getting your teeth clean. No thinking about the past or future; just being while brushing one tooth at a time. Try it and see how simple it can be and recognize that what the mirror shows you is only an image of you. Don't assume and superimpose the false belief that you are only this mere image of the Self. Do the same when you are dressing up or making coffee. Do not allow your mind to be somewhere else. Focus fully on the task at hand. See to it that your mind is always correlating with your actions and ensure that there is no chatter inside your head. And, if there is a thought wondering, let it pass by just like a cloud in a blue sky, or the wave on a calm lake with an image of a full moon.

Along with good habits, we have developed many undesired habits, which cause us pain and suffering. Judging, comparing, doubting, assuming, shaming either ourselves or others are just a few examples. We gossip about others and we gossip about ourselves. There are times when we indulge in excessive eating, television watching, and so on. That brings on guilt and the shaming and blaming and the old pain comes back repeatedly causing us to suffer. Curtail your bad habits and replace them with healthy ones and the suffering will evaporate from your life just like the snow in the sun. Always recognize that there is a time for fun and pleasure, as well as time filled with responsibility and rest. A healthy balance creates healthy thoughts and a healthy body. And always save time for a short meditation and conscious breathing.

One of the most common and most destructive habits is excessive thinking. There is a constant chatter inside our heads. Either we are thinking about the future or the past. We repeat the same thoughts, some true and some untrue, over and over every day and believe them and create our own stories making them our reality upon which we act and see the world.

Did you know that you think about 10,000 thoughts a day? Of those, only 2,000 have any use for your daily existence. No wonder that we are exhausted most of the time. All that constant thinking creating problems and then trying to solve them.

Go deeper within, search what habits are preventing and possibly sabotaging you from achieving your goals. This may take a while as there can be several. Write them down and rather than trying to eliminate the bad habits, try to replace them with good ones that will benefit you and lift you to a higher level of positive thinking, stable balance, and better, healthier results.

This stage is one of the most important and I ask that you to be kind and patient with yourself.

Take it one step at a time.

We are habitual creatures by nature. Unless we are conscious, aware, and mindful constantly, we will slip into old habits. Be aware of your surroundings and your environment and do not allow yourself to fall back to the old routines. And, if you do, which is perfectly OK and normal, simply guide yourself with loving compassion back on track.

The most important message and life-changing experience is making meditation/contemplation a part of your life.

> How can you see your Star
> When the ocean of your Being is covered with ripples?
> How can you hear the Answer
> When your mind is in turmoil?

WHAT HAS MEDITATION TAUGHT ME

Solitude and silence brought me to a place of serenity I have never experienced in life before. Suddenly, there were no questions or obstacles in my life. I lived daily in a relaxed, knowing state having absolute FAITH. When something did not work out as I imagined (expected) it, I would thank the Universe for letting me know that it is time for meditation. Recognizing that I was falling into the bad habit of assuming an outcome of a situation or a performance, leading me to suffer, I developed a state of mind in which I only saw light and the possibility of expanding my consciousness in every situation. I always try to identify and eliminate whatever attitude and behaviour, such as fear, blame, or shame might be influencing my decision-making.

The peace and lightness slowly disappeared as I returned into regular daily life and some bad habits. I first started to shorten and later skip my meditations from time to time. Even though I was meditating, I was constantly seeking the light and love I felt that December of 2015 which was eluding me. I wanted to reach the Divine Love and light that embraced me with a life-changing experience and helped me suddenly realize that I was a part of a much bigger picture and that what I believed to be was truly only a puppet on a string run by body/mind conditioned by patterns, habits, and beliefs.

Once you dissolve your mind and body into the space, let go of fear and trust the Universe to support and guide you there is a sudden connection with the Source of such immense energy fueled by love that you will know instantly that you have come home. This experience can only be true when you forsake your mind and body, the Ego and pride. As soon as a thought enters the field, the connection to the Divine disappears and the mind takes over to govern, often returning one to suffering.

In the past, when I was standing at a fork in the road only seldom did my mind make the right decision and lead me to the right path. A mind is a wonderful tool for working, but when in doubt the best solution is to sit quietly in a dark or dim space and allow the light to enter; waiting quietly for the sign that reveals the appropriate answer to get to our destination. These messages come from the heart and from the soul and, in the beginning, we can only hear and understand them in stillness and silence. Later, we will learn that our mind may receive certain messages which we can slowly learn to understand and decipher even in other circumstances. Life becomes a wonderful experience as we recognize that everything is working in support of the Being.

I have learned that every one of us holds a dream inside. Sometimes, we ignore the impulses or make choices which unfortunately delay our true callings, but the Universe will relentlessly keep reminding us time after time. Learning to understand the cosmic energy of the planets, the movement of the Moon and the Sun through astrology, I am learning to understand myself a little more.

The nudges become stronger and more frequent with age and suddenly there is this feeling inside me that will not allow me to move. This may be a certain thought or an idea that I hold inside, there may be a talent inside me that I have not yet discovered and tapped into that wants to come out like a flower in the spring that is trying so hard to reach the sun. Like the seed planted in the ground can become a tree and bring beauty and fruit, so could our dreams and desires light up this world and help others heal and find beauty and joy.

Through meditation, one can hear and feel these messages loud and clear and, when the full trust and Faith take over, the force of knowing will reveal much deeper Truth. It cannot be comprehended by the mind, this is beyond our mind.

The meditations become sweet like a delicacy. It is an exploration of a new realm Higher Self guiding us and introducing us to new dimensions without limits. Time and space disappear into stillness when meditating. In the beginning, it is difficult to comprehend what meditation is all about. But, as we learn to connect with the Source and the center of our being through meditation, we become fully aware not only of what is happening within us, but also our surroundings become part of us, connecting us to one wholeness. There is a flow, an energy, that we are a part of and as we allow this energy to guide us, life becomes much easier, kinder, and slower to understand and enjoy.

GRACE-BLESSING-RELEASE

In the beginning in 2015, I had to hire a personal assistant because I suffered from phobias, anxiety, and a fear of not knowing who and where I was. I needed help to get me through the day.

I remember anger turning to rage inside me. There were times I would scream and cry into the pillow. I was angry and in pain, both physically, as well as in mental anguish. Not able to do the things I loved so much, like play golf, go skiing, or be involved in the community made me resent everyone else who was having fun. My mind did not work properly with my brain affected by medication. The kidneys were failing and I was in denial, not ready to accept the Truth. Standing in the shower, I cried a river of tears and weeping like the whale in the ocean, asked God to take me and let me die. I did not want to live anymore, I did not want to continue a life filled with pain and suffering. I did not want to be a human being limited and dependent on others.

That angry, fearful, suffering person finally died, that is true today. Her death started a new life. I hardly ever get angry or afraid now and before I allow such emotions to take over, I quickly recognize the pattern and take a time out. I always start with a grounding through attention to my breathing. Only then do I calmly consider the situation and face each emotion. Facing the feelings allows me to recognize the root of the conflict; asking myself who is experiencing these emotions and questioning if they are real or superficial. Recognizing that the ego has once again taken over reshaping my identity brings me back to the Source, where clarity comes naturally in stillness, permitting me to see the whole picture. I simply breathe through the perceived discomfort and let it pass, just like the cramps I often experience in my legs and feet. Relaxation and conscious breathing allow the muscles to naturally release the tightness and the cramp eases and slowly disappears.

With my new habits, I noticed some friends, thinking that I became different, mysterious, and no longer fit in, slowly disappearing from my life. Even some family members felt threatened by the new me and ridiculed and voiced their discontent. I simply let them be and continued with the transformation.

I was changing! Other people noticing my transformation was a priceless bonus which gave me a feeling of joy. Knowing and trusting that the choices were and continued being the right ones, helped reveal the happy Me. No matter the situation, I now feel great being who I am, without the need to pretend or to force anything or trying to be accepted.

Another change in my life that I happily welcomed was eliminating watching television and reading or listening to the news. I hardly ever watch TV anymore, only to keep my husband company once in a while. I prefer to spend my time and energy reading, singing, dancing, writing, or listening to an e-book or just contemplating through meditation. I love my long daily walks in nature bird watching and enjoying the beauty all around me. Every moment seems to offer an opportunity to find something new about myself I wasn't aware of before. Being mindful and aware of my thoughts and actions allows me to live life to the fullest.

Nature suddenly answers many if not all of my questions. Deeper thoughts have altered my attitude towards life and death. Words from the past slowly lose their meaning and are replaced by a new vocabulary or vibration only. Various spiritual self-help books surprised me with new lessons and taught me new ways of breaking a mental block that was holding me from a deeper and further realization of the Self. When I heard a guru or a philosopher whose teachings made sense to me while browsing on YouTube, I would go ahead and purchase their books and read their teachings and used them to learn more about who I am.

If you allow the Universe to be your friend and listen to the advice and see the signs that the Universe sends you, life becomes easier and so much more fun.

I am not afraid of being myself and speaking the truth. The anxieties which kept me tense and under incredible stress affecting my blood pressure and the wellness of the transplanted kidney dissolved as I became calmer and happier. The voice in the back of my head whispering and doubting disappeared altogether, allowing me to live in harmony with the HERE AND NOW.

I've learned that the worst tyrant who caused the most pain in my whole life was my own mind. As a result, I have discovered how to shed the shackles and the chains holding me a prisoner and find the pattern.

There are MANY kinds of thinking.

The working mind is activated by a thought while we are studying, learning a new project or song or dance step. This is a part of growing and creating deeper memories and attaining knowledge. This also applies to daily activities such as walking, cooking, writing, eating, and all normal daily tasks.

1. METHOD ILLUSTRATING NEW DEFINITIONS

M = ethod
I = llustrating
N = ew
D = efinitions

2. MATERIALIZING INTELLIGENCE'S NEW DISCOVERIES

M = aterializing
I = ntelligence's
N = ew
D = iscoveries

Silent Mind

In meditation, when I allow the body to relax and the mind sink into the emptiness the most profound experience penetrates my being and I know I am home.

3. MIRACLE'S IMPULSE TO A NOBLE DESTINY

<u>M</u> = iracle's
<u>I</u> = mpulse to a
<u>N</u> = oble
<u>D</u> = estiny

The <u>"thinking mind"</u> is the culprit who, ever so shrewdly, puts the shackles back on and slowly tightens the leash. Only to mislead me ever so cleverly to the pit and then pulls me mercilessly to the bottom of the dragon's den full of poisonous snakes and other scary creatures. And, the pain and sorrow replay over and over again.

<u>Thinking mind = time</u>

<u>Past or</u>
<u>Future</u>

4. MEMORY INDUCED NOISE DECEIVER

<u>M</u> = emory
<u>I</u> = nduced
<u>N</u> = oise
<u>D</u> = eciever

Whenever I get lost in the sea of thought, I look at what it is that I am searching for. In a few weeks, my mind and I are good friends again and I am the master and the mind is my helper. Making change fun creates a lightness and when things get a little tough, I know that it is time for me to

RE - COGNIZE
RE - ALIZE
RE - ALIGN
RE - STORE
RE - INTEGRATE

the peace and love within the being and eliminate the feeling of separateness.

I know that you too will find many new discoveries and shutting one door will open thousands of others with new friends, new opportunities, and new learning of deeper knowing.

FOCUS
Breathe
CONCENTRATE
Breathe
EMPTY YOUR MIND
Breathe
VISUALIZE
Breathe
ALWAYS LOVE
Breathe

Say yes and the Divine's miracles will start appearing instantly.

Today, I fly alone all over the world, I walk alone at night in safe places, I am not afraid to talk to strangers about the magical 3 Cs to **ALICELAND**. The recognition of the chance that I meet a stranger at a perfect time at a perfect place to exchange our energies and possibly learn something new. Sharing the miracle of the chance of any moment to recognize the truth of who we are, allowing us to adjust our perception and attitude towards life itself and grant us the choice to follow. Sometimes that change is subtle, yet many times it can be a profound awakening and experiencing the beauty of existence and life itself is the most satisfying moment for myself and often for the listener as well. I enjoy each conversation and love to hear people's stories and watch their eyes light up when they learn how to eliminate suffering from their lives and replace it with health, peace, and joy.

WHO YOU THINK YOU ARE

When you look in the mirror, who do you see?

The image looking at you is exactly that; only an IMAGE.

This image is formed from your thoughts and emotions and memories throughout your lifetime. Your parents from birth have been teaching you all they knew, you then went to school, made friends. All these memories of love, fear, pain, anger, hurts, etc. are stored in that image. It is always changing, always different.

Your brain has created the "me," Ego, the image to find security. The Ego is never fully satisfied, always wanting to be different, creating conflict in the brain. The fear of its existence separates us from the rest. It is not seeing the truth but perceiving the image from memory, therefore, living in an illusion.

Alice Pesta

IMAGE OF WHO WE THINK WE ARE

- EGO
- PAST
- FUTURE

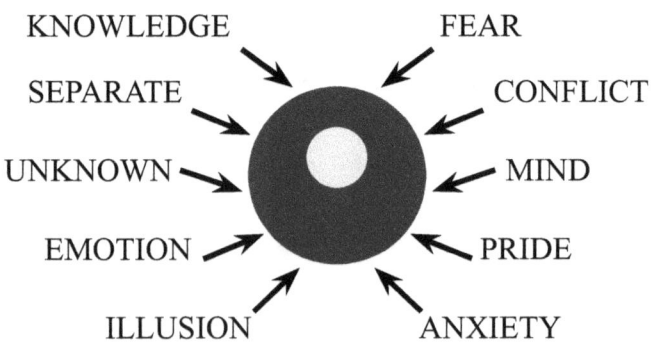

- ALWAYS CHANGING
- NEVER FULLY SATISFIED
- WANTING TO BE DIFFERENT
- PERCEIVING

BE WHO YOU ARE

Are we sabotaging ourselves?

To meet the SELF, you must be

- **PRESENT**
- **STILL**
- **QUIET**

That what you are not

Take a close look at who we are not on the previous page.

For thousands of years, the human race has been evolving and now man is planning a trip to Mars. Is it necessary to travel that far to truly know oneself? It seems to me that we have lost touch with our true inner self and are looking further from the source and suffering the same or even more than the caveman. Are we capable of truly knowing the complexity of our self and answer without any doubt any and all questions? Hardly.

The true self is always present and always now. The self never changes.

One must come to the point when suddenly there is a feeling for perception without any motive direction. That perception is LOVE, that perception is INLIGHTENMENT*, that perception is you.

*In my opinion, we are all enlightened from birth, when we take our first breath, as we would not be seen otherwise. But, throughout our lifetime we build a wall or a thick veil in our hearts that is preventing us to "INLIGHTEN" from within and allow the two to merge creating peace and harmony and the SELF to be present.

My future depended on it. Somewhere inside, there was a little voice, a little quiver, a vibration saying...this is it...I must change! My whole body/mind felt this energy vibrating through my spine into the neck and my brain was just tingling with fear, doubt, despair. It was as if some other power from above was warning, whispering ... be careful.

And, then, I asked myself, "Who am I? Who is this person I know nothing of? I want to have myself back again."

My journey was just beginning, and this is what I learned.

I am enlightened
As any form to be found
Is lit with the Divine...
It's the light inside
which is crucial to find.

BE WHO YOU ARE

•SELF

•BREATH **THE PRESENT**

•ENERGY

•KNOWING

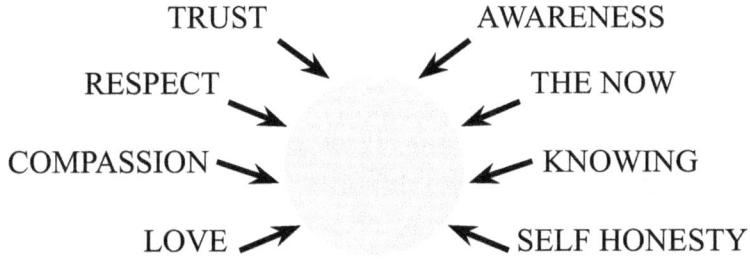

- ARE WE SELF-SABOTAGING OURSELVES?
- BE PRESENT
- BE STILL
- BE QUIET

One must come to the point when suddenly there is a feeling for perception without any motive direction.

That perception is love, that perception is intelligence, that perception is you.

To be completely aware of the full reach of mind, one must be conscious at the deepest level of the totality of consciousness.

STICK TO IT

Meditate on it, take long walks in nature.

Ponder on it.

Investigate each angle of possibility.

Be mindful.

Hold onto that chance to learn and recognize deeply who you are. There may not come another one, and if it does, it will never be the same. Deep inside your body, hear the whisper within. Do it for me. Feeling it in every core - DOING what you were doing for the past twenty, thirty, seventy years is not working anymore. That game is over and there is a new game, a new player, new strategies with brand new rules.

POWER OF FORGIVENESS

HEALING STARTS WITH FORGIVENESS

The most effective way to start any healing and to find happiness is forgiveness. I call happiness the shortcut to bliss. Once we recognize what is blocking our way to the light, replace it with joy in each moment and start releasing the unnecessary weight and conditioning. Happiness, love, and compassion will embrace us from within.

Our goals will become attainable and our inner wisdom will guide us where we know we are longing to be. It is important to realize the POWER OF BREATH. Life can be very simple once we gain clarity of what is most important for our being. By elimination, we will recognize that which we are trying to reach, is within us, and we do not even have to leave the chair we are sitting on.

Step 1. Become **PRESENT**

Step 2. Take THREE DEEP BREATHS
  a. Deep cleansing breath
  b. Deeper release tension breath
  c. Relaxing into emptiness breath

Looking at our existence from what keeps us alive, it is necessary to recognize that our basic needs are the fuel to our vehicle we call BODY. It has been recommended to eat five small meals a day. You may have heard a statement "You are what you eat.

It is wise to choose light, easily digested meals to allow us to perform the actions we choose to manifest. If I were to do strenuous work, then, of course, I would need a heavier, more substantial meal. If I am going to be running, I then need a meal which is high in nutrition and vitamins and electrolytes, etc. If I am a sumo wrestler, my diet would be way different than that of a ballerina. What a wonderful world we live in to be able to learn anything with a push of a button on the computer keyboard.

Step 3. Acknowledge the existence of our body/mind

For making the right decision, it is necessary to have a healthy mind. If our days are filled with negative, worrisome, judgmental thoughts, our mood becomes darker and our days seem to be difficult. By allowing the thought to shift from a heavy, negative pattern of perceiving the world through a dark glass of judgment, comparison, anger, etc. into a light glass of accepting, compassion, and positive attitude, we could suddenly see the rainbow and the pot of gold waiting for us.

It is important to feed our mind with healthy food.

The best food for thought is silence. In silence, we can discern what is true and what is an illusion; which thought comes from LOVE and which thought is the byproduct of FEAR. In other words, when we are working on a project or have a meeting to attend and are prepared and are aligned with our intention, there is a feeling of oneness and lightness of action just like swimming without any resistance.

Fear, on the other hand, will create an uneasy feeling and emotion, filling our mind with doubt and uncertainty. We feel separated from the Source which blocks the flow of creative energy resulting in conflicts within oneself.

Whether we are working or playing, our mind sends the body a message manifesting our desire. There are different ways of using our brain. Let's imagine ourselves driving a car with a friend. While taking the trip, we are enjoying each other's company talking and paying attention to the conversation. We are not really paying conscious attention to the driving or the surroundings. Yet, we safely reach our destination following the "programmed thinking." The same thing happens while we are creating art or fully applying our mind to playing an instrument. We lose the perception of time and action and become total beings. Being "in the zone," we experience the fact that we are not the doer, but that there is an energy flowing through us. We let the mind sink into the depth beyond the heart into the soul and watch miracles manifest through us.

Resting the mind has become a luxury for humans, usually only existing in deep sleep. In the last twenty years, the amount of impulses from the outer world keeps our mind constantly occupied with new thoughts and new desires. It is important to learn how to have a quiet moment and allow the mind to rest in silence or with the help of soft music, guided meditation, or a mantra.

Step 4. Understand the power of thought

Now that we recognize the basis of our existence, we can focus on what makes our life difficult. Often, we feel frustrated when our desires are not being met. It is the ego whose demands and desires need constant attention to feel its existence. Assuming others know what we need and want creates frustration, anger, and blame. These feelings then produce tension and stress in the body. Long-term stress can be the cause of an illness, later turning into chronic disease.

Accordingly, I suggest that every day as often as needed we slow down, take the sacred three breaths, and count our blessings.

Recognize what is not aligning
Realize if the perception of the situation is true
Detach if the reality is beyond your control
Allow and Accept eliminating resistance

Become a student and learn from life itself. Nothing ever stays the same and things change. Letting go of yesterday's memory frees the heart and soul to fully shine within and enlighten the whole world today, opening the door invisible to us when we let the ego govern. Flexibility, forgiveness, non-attachment are the vehicles to joy and compassion.

Start with forgiving yourself first and most of all. Let Self-love and Self-acceptance guide your being. Allow gratitude to be your attitude.

CHANGE OF ONE'S ATTITUDE

MAY

CHANGE THE ATTITUDE

OF THE WORLD

BE THE ONE

CHOICE WORKSHEET

Take each question very seriously and before you answer, focus on what you need and want now.

How can I **be** happy?

The word **BE** is the **KEY** word in this sentence.

It is time to BE a human being, not a human doing living life built of patterns and conditions.

What is your reality at this moment?
_____
_____
_____

(i.e. I feel mistreated and I can't do anything right)

Contemplate that.
_____
_____
_____

(i.e. who is feeling this reality and is it true?)

If it is real, what we are being taught and conditioned to believe, then who has the authority to teach and condition us?

_____
_____
_____

(i.e. I can question everything I experience whether or not it resonates with me)

Are these authorities living a blissful and a happy life?

_____
_____
_____

(i.e. what others may experience as bliss may be pain for me)

Is it possible that there is another approach to life, to thinking and to living?

_____
_____
_____

(i.e. I trust that I have the power to revise my life)

What is true for me now?

_____
_____
_____

(i.e. I am not consistent)

How did I get here?

_____
_____
_____

(i.e. I make the choice based on emotion)

Where do I want to go?

_____
_____
_____

(i.e. I want to be free from suffering)

How do I get there?

_____
_____
_____

(i.e. I stick with my simple agenda, I align with what makes me happy)

THINK UNTHINKABLE

DO UNDOABLE

SPEAK UNSPEAKABLE

BE IGNITABLE

EMPTINESS

> *"Emptiness ultimately means that genuine reality is empty of any conceptual fabrication that could attempt to describe what it is."*
>
> Khenpo Tsultrim Gyamtso

Be conscious, mindful and fully present with the beauty of nature. Calgary is now wearing a beautiful colourful coat with countless shades of greens, yellows, oranges, and reds, saying goodbye to another summer and getting ready for a long winter. I adore this time of year and try to be outside with nature and get inspired by the short autumn we usually experience in Alberta, Canada. It is never long enough, as it takes only a few frosty days followed by strong west winds from the Rockies or the icy North Territories and all the colour disappears, bringing a new stage of life in the wink of an eye. Sometimes, without warning, the whole city is covered with an unexpected gift of a pure white coat of snow.

Thinking about my life, I identify myself more and more with nature and its continuous flow of living and dying. The spring is wild and full of life, birth and rapid growth. The first six years of human life forms the pattern in the development of thinking, beliefs and attitudes towards the self and others. Just like the garden needs to be tended, so does our mind. Development of our psyche and consciousness and physical being demands constant close loving tenderness to bloom into its full beauty and abundance.

Unfortunately, in today's society, living in a very material world with demands of instant gratification, it is difficult to avoid some patterns, habits, and desires. From birth, children learn their first habits and patterns from their family, their heritage, religious practices, and later are influenced by television and now social media. With smart-phones and iPads, our brains are seldom still. The mind is constantly busy with either thinking or in a conversation of several voices within.

Always busy with our heads full of thoughts about the past or the future, what must be done or what has not manifested yet, one desire follows another, seldom satisfied, always with a critic in the background. This inner noise avoids the call of the soul, yet it is the soul which is the bridge between the body/mind and the Source allowing us to see the whole picture of reality. This leaves us walking with many shades covering our eyes, missing the whole beauty and purpose of our existence.

Trying to fit in, we imitate our parents, classmates, teachers, coaches, movie stars, singers or other celebrities, as we try to be accepted in a social environment. Less and less time is spent alone in silence. Only in the stillness and silence can we discover the beauty and fullness as well as the innocence each one of us holds within.

With the mind now conditioned and the constant chatter inside the head full of thoughts and arguments about the past or future dreaming, judging, comparing, and seeking ways to satisfy the hunger and desire for love which we naturally crave, the image of who we are is based on a false belief of what was said to us or what we have learned at school.

What we think, believe, and judge in the mirror creates a conflict within, constantly strengthening the illusionary me, the Ego. It is, therefore, necessary to recognize where the thought came from and then make the choice to either feed the thought further into an image or, if it is not relevant or true, then let it go by just like a single wave in the ocean and let it dissolve into the water.

Chapter 3

Just like leaves turning to golden in colour, so those of us facing middle age try to hold onto each leaf and outer beauty of our image. A few of us will go to every possible avenue to prevent the natural process of aging and maturity influenced by constant images from magazines, commercials, posters, television, beauty clinics and so on.

Even though this is harvest time in nature, many of us find the golden age to be rather dark and gloomy and full of uncertainty. Just like the cold rain, sleet, and heavy winds blow away all leaves so they allow gloomy thoughts to mask all memories of the beauty and innocence of youth. Sadly, instead of looking back with a smile and sense of fun, many stay in the darkness of the past drama and tragedies. Sometimes, it is an old argument in a family or with a friend that is irrelevant twenty years later but resurrected only for the benefit of the bruised Ego which needs to reinforce the pride that is holding the door to love and happiness shut.

Cynicism, bitterness and despair can take over one's mind as the circle of life reaches another stage and so many carry all the perceived injustices and sorrows of the past on their shoulders, not allowing themselves to enjoy the beauty of life in the present.

Harvest time and thanksgiving provide an opportunity to review and see what we are leaving behind, the consequences of our choices and actions which brought us to where we are now and to plan the next phase of our existence. Hopefully, by this stage, we will see clearly which patterns and habits have helped us to feel satisfied and which have brought us to despair and will proceed cautiously.

THE ONLY REAL MISTAKES
WE MAKE...ARE THE ONES
FROM WHICH WE LEARN
NOTHING...

Once again, it is important to recognize where we feel stuck and what we have control of changing. With more time on our hands, we may discover meditation, slow things down and learn new possible ways to create stability and freedom in our lives.

Once we decide to take our lives into our own hands and recognize that our perception of what we want and what we see becomes transparent, many of us take the quest to find truth, as it becomes crucial in finding stability.

-                    GET **CLEAR** ABOUT
                              WHAT
-                 YOU **NEED** TO ACCOMPLISH

                                   VS

-              WHAT YOU **SHOULD** ACCOMPLISH

THROUGH THE CONNECTION TO YOUR HIGHER SELF

Nature and the universe manage all energy perfectly. Do not let your mind deceive you into prematurely letting go of the dreams of your childhood. There is time to start a new process of learning and creating skills to complete our life task and to serve the whole community as well as to fulfill our talents. Knowing this fact, beware of your emotional body as well as the thinking body and search the root of each conflict holding you back with the gift of silent stillness. Recognize the imbalance within which brings on the suffering and prevents us from reaching our full flourishment.

I have fully detoxed myself from most drugs. The biggest killer and the most destructive drug of all was my addiction to thinking. It was thought which was the toxin poisoning my mind without my consciousness. Ever so subtly, the beast of desire took over to feed its need for more pleasure and then lead me to destruction, not once, but most of my life, until I recognized the pattern and the root of my suffering.

Without thought, there was no reason to question what was real and true. I knew that I was real, I knew that I AM, I knew that I had a choice to either continue and walk the same path to self-destruction or to focus on the heart and stillness to lead me home to joy and serenity.

Once you are comfortable with the reality that you are the conscious awareness, allow your true being to pass the image of the form. Discover the limitless reality beyond the form, the clarity of what is real becomes striking and you will see the absurdity of your previous beliefs, patterns, habits, and attachments originating in a lie superimposed on the human race.

Each moment of every day, I am ready to face miracles, challenges, and impulses as they present themselves, and breathe through them while allowing them to flow through me. With a loving understanding of who I am and what is happening, I learn to accept everything as it really is without any judgment or attachment and continue to experience life without fear or threat to my existence and being.

If you are feeling pain, despair, and suffering, if you are at the end of your rope, let go and allow yourself to fall into the unknown.

Drop into nothingness, disappear...dig below the bottom if

you must. Let the bullying mind die and delete the stories in the program within your brain. Look fear straight into the eye, face it, and stay with it with conscious breathing. It will dissolve into space as soon as you recognize that it is unfounded and unreal, an illusion.

Without desires, empty, silent, and complete life turns 180 degrees from nothing to everything. Learning not to assume and not to expect things, actions, and behaviours of others to fit the perception of what should be, letting go of attachments to all forms, frees one to go beyond that which is believed to be true (the illusion), when in reality anything in temporary structure is unreal.

The pie of life is the sweetest when enjoyed with gratitude, humility and accepting the miracle of being a human. Recognizing, understanding and accepting the fact that we are not the doers, each day becomes a great movie in which we are the directors and actors with the screen in one.

Through practice and affirmation of the new reality, we can achieve anything in life. Fully focused on the Self and being true to our heart in stillness without any attachments we will find the path home. Just like a plane flying any distance from one place to another, when it veers off course, the pilot will realign the plane's direction to stay within the parameters and land at the desired destination. It is most important to keep aligned with our goals and stay aware of all distractions and unnecessary disturbances.

Stay empty, formless, and always shine in your true being. Bon voyage.

The Third C of Aliceland

CHANGE

EGO

FREEDOM

JOY

EGO

Changes are constant all around and within us.
The only thing that stays constant is that which cannot be seen.

Ego, the me, the I, is the one and only that needs to be taken care of. Our ego, which is an image created by our mind from the memory of feelings, sensations, and perceptions, is the wall preventing us from recognizing who our true self is. The mind is conditioned and built to listen to the Ego and react upon its desire, never to be satisfied because it is separate from the Source.

Going deeper into our psyche and spending time in solitude and silence can bring profound discoveries when learning who we truly are. This pathless road to knowing the TRUTH is a beautiful odyssey from oneself to ONESELF. This involves many baby steps and many leaps and days or weeks standing still. Learning from the planets above us and walking a similar journey here on this planet Earth, we too turn back and re-do, re-learn the best ways to overcome and release the challenges which are hard and painful. But, the pain and chaos we feel inside become the ignition to recognize that we must be active in realizing what is the root cause of our ache. The change starts within us.

Learning to love myself and to honour my body taught me to slow down. I was experimenting with new ways of conscious breathing. That led to slowing down my thinking and I became aware of the body-mind connection. The colours of the world suddenly became brighter, the sun was shining longer, and sometimes I felt a splurge of happiness from looking at the sunset, or a beautiful piece of art.

To understand the meaning of the word love, we must first understand the depth of the feeling of absolute peace and compassion within us. This love that heals is not sexual or possessive. This love is the LOVE OF ACCEPTANCE and SURRENDER to the Being. There is no judgment, there is no thought, there is only the feeling of peace and Grace.

I have learned that emotions are a very powerful force in my decisions for the next action. In order to feel happy and stable, I need to be in a position where there is no conflict in the brain. Always questioning the reason for any discomfort or too much excitement, I have created this solution to see clearly how to stay within the stream of constant joy

E – MOTION	=	E - NERGY
Time + space		L I F E
Past - SPACE – Future		E G O (me)
------NOW------		HIGHER SELF
thought/mind		C O L L E C T I V E
IMAGE		STILLNESS & SILENCE
EGO		I M P U L S E (through stillness)
DEATH		SELF - REALIZATION

The Ego shifts from the side of self-center and selfishness and recognizes the whole and the other side to expand and embrace the heart of the collective. These changes are subtle, yet very profound, helping the perspective for the future to seem brighter and easier. We start seeing the rainbow, we hear the birds sing, and we look at the world from the eye of the perceiver.

Gradually, as we slow down, stay relaxed and calm, avoid resistance, the image of the (me) ego dissolves (dies) into the awareness. In Awareness, we realize the sacredness of silence and stillness and allow life to be breathed into us witnessing miracles through the eyes on the screen of space we are in.

To recognize the reality of the I - AM - NESS is the gateway to fully understanding the phrase "I AM in the world, but not of the world." This leads to realizing that consciousness is also illusionary, allowing the expansion of the mind.

I caught myself not worrying about this or that, my whole thinking became less active, less chaotic, I trusted the Universe and life, recognizing that there is a driver driving my car and I have not yet crashed. I became a passenger without commenting or assuming what was happening around me. Growing more confident of the fact that life supports life always and under all circumstances, reassures my belief daily that there is a reason why I am here right now. The mind stops to judge, compare, or change anything. Things, actions, people were coming and going, and I would simply enjoy them. All around me was peace.

Finally, I let go.

Faith is the force that gets me going. Trust and faith in the Universe and the connection with the Divine is the energy behind everything that is. All that I have achieved is through this unknown energy that we are all blessed with.

FREEDOM

From the voices, free of undesired patterns, addictions and desires, freedom is the highest sense of security within the Self.

Through meditation, I became more and more aware of the five senses.

1. Smell
2. Sight
3. Touch
4. Taste
5. Hearing

As I expanded my knowledge through learning how to listen to my body, I recognized other sensations and feelings, which I previously took for granted and never paid any attention to. Did you know that touch can be divided into four distinct experiences such as pressure, temperature, pain, and itch?

We have the ability to feel through our senses the difference between cold and heat or the different vibrations in sound like wind or the water in the ocean. Altogether, there are twenty-one senses described and accepted by many researchers. I believe that with the influx of new research coming to our knowledge and understanding we may find solutions to our suffering and learn how to expand our consciousness.

Walks in nature became a new experience. In the beginning, it was such a drag and I had to really push myself, but as time went on I realized that I was looking forward to the fresh air. Once I became tired of the regular routine, I found a new path of discovery. Staying mindful (aware) at all times, I learned how to meditate through the walks and allowed myself to integrate all the new teachings of being one with the universe as a whole. I had amazing results in listening to the ideas coming to me through the vibration I felt through my whole being. There were surges of new inspirations and I learned to carry a mini booklet with a pencil to write them all down and create reality from that which was just a thought a few minutes before.

I would explore the feelings and vibrations of trees and flowers and everything was in harmonious and loving oneness. I would catch myself singing and dancing with the marigolds, daisies, peonies, and daffodils. Hugging trees and trying to listen to their whispers became my favourite habit.

I allowed my mind to wonder and become childlike. Wondering, loving, laughing, learning, I created my own world based on acceptance, love, and joy. Everything fit in harmony and there was peace, serenity, and happiness all around me.

FREEDOM from the Monkey Mind and enslaved body to the mind was a BIG VICTORY. Without television or newspapers, I had no idea what was going on in the world and I did not care. It did not concern me. My main goal was to go through the transformation to find that which made me happy and kept balance within myself.

Always focused to stay centred and not be swayed by emotions, desires, or expectations which I found and recognized were the gateway to my suffering, I learned to live by a few new rules:

MY PLAN IS NO PLAN

MY PROBLEM IS NOT TO HAVE A PROBLEM

I AM HAPPY TO MAKE MYSELF HAPPY

These three changes have made my life so much more

fun. I do not mind if a plan changes, because any plan can be changed at the spur of the moment. And I have learned in the last fifty-some years that it is much better to experience a delay on a flight or experience a broken car or a household gadget than having high blood pressure or losing myself in anger or frustration, blaming whatever could be blamed, only to avoid recognizing that the problem starts and ends in my own mind.

With this new attitude, it was easy to let the life flow at ease day by day. Of course, with all the travelling, the need to eat, finding shelter, and other basic needs, one must have an essential plan to survive. But, those become simple pleasures to be included on a "to do" list. Each morning, the day fully opens its arms inviting me to discover new miracles in every step to realize who I AM. There is so much of myself I still do not know and that is why I am excited to find out the whole potential still undiscovered inside of me.

Life is full of surprises and I love to watch how it unfolds. The story just keeps going and sometimes the end is better than a fairytale. As soon as I sense that the mind is trying to complain about what is, I take a deep breath, and then another. Sometimes, five or six breaths are needed to slow down my thoughts and the thinking pattern that still resonates from the past trying to argue with what is and trying to persuade the mind what the reality should be like. I realize how silly it is….and then usually I burst out laughing. There is no problem, and there never was a problem; just a different approach and attitude to the whole situation can make the glass perfectly full. Half is full of water and the other is full of air. How wonderful. Since we are living beings made up of the five elements of earth, fire, water, air, and space we need air to breathe. So, the glass is full of two elements water and air, otherwise, we might drown :)

And to make myself happy? That is the easiest one most of the time. If I am not happy, who can be happy for me? Really? Well, I guess I can call my friend and ask her to be happy for me for a day or two that I am tired of being happy. But, we all know that is absurd. So, instead, I choose to be happy for myself. And if at times a difficult situation arises, I ensure to at least be content with understanding fully what I am perceiving and how my mind is processing each impulse from everything that is happening around and within me.

Realization of the fact that I am being breathed into and therefore allowed to be alive is the answer to the first question to understand how to recognize the shrewdness of the mind to trick itself, to a useless argument of the illusionary imagination.

And, if I need help, I have plenty of gadgets to help me. With meditation to get grounded, slow down and allow the vibration to resonate with the Universe, I eliminate the feeling of separation from the Source. As long as we are mindful and one with the Source there is peace and balance.

Music is another great tool and sometimes I just get up and dance and shake off the tension and loosen the knots that I have allowed to build up inside my body. It feels marvellous to work out a sweat and if there is any anger or feelings of frustration creeping in, let them flow out of your system. Do not stuff them to the bottom of the pressure cooker. The consequences could be deadly and the damage difficult to repair.

Allowing the feelings and sensation to simply flow through without any resistance, labels, or attachments makes the day go by smoothly and without any unnecessary tension. Learning the fact that I am just simply alive gives me the freedom to explore the world as a witness.

With today's ability to find anything online I have listened to some of the most amazing people on YouTube and podcasts. The Universe has no reservations and offers you anything you wish for. Do not limit yourself with your doubts allowing the mind to start to create stories. If you allow doubt and fear into your house, you can never find true peace. Love is built on trust. Allow yourself to be that which you are and stop seeking the imagination of your mind.

INLIGHTMENT

We are enlightened—
The forms to be seen
Lit through Divine.
It is the light inside
That is crucial to find
To be One with Her all the time

JOY

When you least anticipate anything to happen, miracles happen; the brilliant light and love will penetrate every cell within you. You become weightless as if your body disappeared into space. The silence will become alive and life will become serene. There is no time, no distance - emptiness turns into pure joy and love. And that is Grace.

Be quiet and sit still. Allow this phenomenon to fully engulf and soak you in this new experience. You have arrived. You are home. You are loved.

You are LOVE itself.

WORKSHEET FOR CHANGE

What do I want now?

_____
_____
_____

(i.e. I want to be fully present from moment to moment)

What has changed in me that I am most proud of

_____
_____
_____

(i.e. my emotions are less dramatic through the three breaths of grounding)

Am I awake or am I asleep?

_____
_____
_____

(i.e. there are times when I catch myself bouncing back to the past, but am able to quickly redirect and realign with the now)

What have I learned controls my thinking pattern?

_____
_____
_____

(i.e. I realized that certain people and situation became real in my mind and forced me to go back to the past)

What is the cause of not reaching my goals?

_____
_____
_____

(i.e. I get easily distracted by external or internal impulses)

How can I best eliminate the cause of not reaching my goals?

_____
_____
_____

(i.e. I will set aside a certain time of day for me time reducing the amount of my project etc.)

What has stillness taught me so far?

_____
_____
_____

(i.e. I have decreased and eliminated many anxieties and fears)

What does happiness mean to me NOW?

_____
_____
_____

(i.e. being satisfied with myself and understand I am on a journey)

What affirmations have been most helpful on my journey?

_____
_____
_____

(i.e. I surrender to the now)

What supports my change the most so far?

_____
_____

(i.e. being aware and present of the NOW)

About the Author

Alice Pesta

Alice Pesta was born in the former communist Czechoslovakia in the City of Krnov on the border with Poland. In 1981 Alice's family emigrated to Canada where she married and lived most of her adult life. In her youth she contracted chronic kidney disease which ultimately resulted in kidney failure, dialysis treatments, two transplants, addiction to prescribed pain killers and a multitude of other medical complications. In coping with the various medical challenges faced by her Alice developed a unique approach to staying positive and productive, Aliceland, which she shares in this book. Alice loves to travel and now spends part of each year between Calgary, Phoenix and Prague all of which she calls home.

Alice recently celebrated her thirtieth wedding anniversary with her husband Lou Pesta and two adult children, Domenic and Nicole.

www.ingramcontent.com/pod-product-compliance
Lightning Source LLC
Chambersburg PA
CBHW070503090426
42735CB00012B/2665